MERRY XMAS DAD.
LOVE FROM
MARK & STACEY.

MORE
Tales of the
OLD GAMEKEEPERS

MORE
Tales of the
OLD GAMEKEEPERS

Brian P. Martin

David & Charles

To Sam Prince and John George,
gone but not forgotten

———————————

Also by Brian Martin and published by David & Charles

Sporting Birds of Britain & Ireland
Birds of Prey of the British Isles
Wildfowl of the British Isles & North-west Europe
The Glorious Grouse
The Great Shoots
Tales of the Old Gamekeepers
Tales of the Old Countrymen

———————————

Illustrations by Philip Murphy

A DAVID & CHARLES BOOK

Copyright © Text: Brian P. Martin 1993

First published 1993
Reprinted 1994

Brian P. Martin has asserted his right to be identified as author of this work
in accordance with the Copyright, Designs and Patents Act 1988.

A catalogue record for this book is available from the British Library

ISBN 0 7153 0057 1

Typeset by Ace Filmsetting Ltd, Frome, Somerset
and printed in Great Britain by Butler & Tanner
for David & Charles
Brunel House Newton Abbot Devon

CONTENTS

KEEPING THE FAITH

His clock is set by Nature
    and has no division of hours,
for both his past and future
    belong to much deeper powers.

In an endless round of seasons
    he knows only dark and light,
cold and warm, wet and dry reasons
    why days are drear or delight.

In youth his passion and strength
    endure against uncertainty,
but with the wisdom of years
    he walks in Nature's harmony.

His furrow is as straight as him,
    his harvest a natural crop;
his wages are paid by Nature
    and his motor will never stop.

BRIAN MARTIN, 1992

INTRODUCTION

After the encouraging reception given to my book *Tales of the Old Gamekeepers*, I was delighted to have the opportunity to unearth another dozen great characters. There was never any fear that I would not find an equally interesting group of men because almost every corner of the kingdom is home to their very special breed. Indeed, my main problem was who to leave out!

Very sadly, two very distinguished keepers, who would definitely have featured, died before I could talk to them in detail. Now the stories of Sam Prince and John George have been lost for ever. Also, several others became too ill or too confused to be interviewed, so their tales have had to be put on hold, pending hoped-for recovery.

My twelve subjects are from widely spaced areas of England, Scotland and Wales, and most of them have worked on several estates at least so between them they have been able to describe life as it was in a total of twenty-five counties, from Forfar to Hampshire, from Anglesey to Suffolk. Most have worked mainly with partridges and pheasants, but some have been chiefly grouse men, enduring the very different rigours of northern moors.

Wherever possible, I have let the characters describe experiences in their own, colourful language. But in some cases dialect has been impossible to put on paper, so this has not been attempted where confusion could result. Indeed, it was sometimes the case that my subjects had to make a special effort so that I could understand. In a few instances we have had to guess at the spelling of a word because neither the story-teller nor I had seen it written down before. Also, it has been necessary to 'interpret' a few expressions which might not travel well, but I am confident that their general meaning is clear. However, what I can only describe as regional innuendo is much more difficult to pin down. Perhaps I should apologise now for any unintentional emphasis.

This time I have decided to give priority to age, so the book starts with 98-year-old Ned Turvey and ends with the 'baby' – 64-year-old Harry Starling. Their retirement ages have varied greatly, and several have continued working well past 80. However, almost without exception they have admitted to me that they can

remember the events of fifty years ago more clearly than those of last week. For example, the price of tobacco in 1929 comes to mind more readily than when the milk bill was last paid. But I suppose this is common to most of us as we pass the halfway mark on life's journey.

In all cases I have given details of pay, clothing and conditions of service. These are often very similar, but I believe important so that both chronological and regional comparisons can be made.

The county list at the head of each chapter does not reflect relative importance, but the order in which the keepers lived there. Each account not only records the highlights of a man's career, but also seeks to impart the flavour of family and social life, from childhood to retirement. Thus, along with descriptions of appointments, war service and medal presentations are simple notes of what was eaten and which pastimes were pursued. Equally important, there are many unique observations of wildlife and comments about the countryside from days which are generally regarded as 'golden'.

Virtually all these men preferred the old ways of working, which were often more in harmony with nature. They have certainly not welcomed increasing commercialisation of sport as estates have struggled to make ends meet, which has put so many men out of work and encouraged a less caring kind of employer. Indeed, in some cases I have been staggered by the dreadful way keepers have been treated. It is hard to believe that such long loyalty to an estate or family can be so undervalued by later generations of owners, even when hard-pressed by recession. Where this has occurred I have been asked not to name names, but I hope the guilty will have a twinge of conscience. Fortunately, lack of acknowledgement of an employee's outstanding service is extremely rare in the shooting world and most of my subjects have made it clear to me that if they were 14 years old they would 'do it all again'.

In researching both gamekeeper books I have discovered a great deal of prejudice against modern keepers generally. 'They don't know they're born' and 'they're all instant headkeepers', are just two comments I have heard on many occasions. But I think such sweeping statements have to be taken with the proverbial pinch of salt because the old ways are seen as better in so many areas of life. My subjects do not really believe that 'career' keepers today are any less motivated than they always were. They are simply the products of changing times and the inevitable drive towards greater efficiency. If the 'old boys' really hated the way things have turned out they would not keep turning up to lend a hand to 'the lad' on shoot days!

Today's young lions are tomorrow's veterans and I have no doubt that they too will have their remarkable stories of changing times with which to beguile others in the next century. In the meantime, both young and old keepers are united in a love of the outdoors and sporting tradition. Their enthusiasm may have meant enduring relative poverty during the early days, but there is no denying the richness of their lives.

BRIAN P. MARTIN
Brook, Surrey

SURVIVOR OF THE TRENCHES

NED TURVEY

STAFFORDSHIRE

When 19-year-old gamekeeper Ned Turvey volunteered for the Army in World War I he was completely unaware of the carnage which lay ahead of him. Now aged ninety-eight, he remains a firm believer in discipline and reflects on the sad decline of the old-fashioned virtues which helped him survive both the terror of the trenches and a lifetime in keepering.

One of seven children, Edward Victor Randolph Turvey (always known as Ned) was born on 20 September 1895, at Hilton Park, near Wolverhampton, where his father was headkeeper for A. L. Vernon for twelve years. His paternal grandfather had been an estate labourer.

At the age of three and a half, Ned went to Essington School – 'all galvanised sheeting, just like the church. We used to walk through the woods to get there. I had a good, firm master. People used to say, "Mr Walker's a very good man – he goes to church on Sunday and prays to the Lord to give him strength to wallop the kids on Monday". Parents don't bother with their children now. It's all too easy.

'Owing to ill health in the family, the doctor advised my parents to leave the house, so in 1900 we moved to Lord Hatherton's estate, between Cannock and Penkridge, where father was headkeeper. Then I went to Cannock National School.

Five-year-old Ned Turvey (extreme right) at a shoot in 1900. His father is far left, holding a gun

'Father was a good provider and we was a happy family. We always went to church and Sunday school and was taught things properly. There was always a rabbit or pigeon to eat and you always had a good garden. Mother was a tiptop cook too – been in gentlemen's service. We 'ad a lot of good soup then and plenty of good bacon. All meat was no price: hip-bone steak just 10d (4p) a pound and sausages 4d a pound – none of these fancy prices now. Meat was much tastier too, with a little bit of fat – that's what you want! Mother always knew what to buy – she 'ad to as there was nine of us in the house with a keeper lodgin'.

'Our lighting was all oil lamps of course, but things improved later on when the Tilley lamp came in. We always burned coal and logs. Even when I got married to Alice in 1921 coal was still only 14/6d a ton, and half a crown to draw it with horse and cart. Now only last week I paid £150 for a ton and half – and that was supposed to be a special price. No – it's all twisted now. When I was a lad, ordinary whisky was only four bob a bottle, but Black Label was 12 shillings.

'Years ago a lad used to bring out the Guns' lunches from Paterson's at Birmingham – everythin' you could want. Then my wife took over, and everybody loved mother's damson jam. Before the first war father used to get Flower's best bitter delivered from Penkridge for 10d a gallon. Even the very best bitter was only shilling a gallon. It came on the train, then the local grocer brought it out.

'Then there was plenty of wildlife of every description, including corncrakes, nightjars and quails. 'Course the vermin was kept down and that made the difference. There it is – the law of the land. And the woods was magnificent with bluebells and daffodils. I remember years later, when they cut all the trees down, I've never seen such a pretty sight as all the foxgloves.'

Because Ned had to walk three miles to school he became very familiar with all the birds and flowers which were still very common. But the daily exercise was never any excuse for slacking. Indeed, when Ned came out of school he often had to help dad on the rearing field. 'I suppose it was education as far as me father was concerned.'

Ned never had any secret ambition while still in education and it was no surprise when he left school, at the age of thirteen years and four months in 1908, to work with his father. 'Everythin' was dead against you then, and in the keepin' world at least you very soon learned that a still tongue was a wise tongue.'

Without motorised transport in relatively isolated rural communities, Ned and his generation rapidly learned to become self-sufficient. And as the doctor had to be paid for his services, many folk had their own remedies for various ailments. Ned has certainly stuck by his. Indeed, as we spoke he noticed that I was looking distinctly uncomfortable because my long car journey had aggravated a back complaint. 'I reckon you've got a touch of lumbago there', he said. 'I've got a good cure for that – always carry a lump of nutmeg about in your pocket. I've got a little bit on me now.' And with that he reached deep into his trousers pocket to produce a little cloth bag, the drawstring of which he unravelled with some difficulty to reveal a piece of nutmeg worn smooth with the years. 'I can guarantee that if ever I forget it I get twinges. 'Course me father had it very bad.'

I asked how his dad had travelled around. 'Oh, he 'ad a bicycle. It'd be a strong one of course – an Ideal – because he was a big chap – eighteen stone. We all 'ad

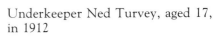

Underkeeper Ned Turvey, aged 17, in 1912

Volunteer for the Great War, aged 19

bikes in them days, soon as we could afford 'em. Mind you, the train service was good then, with lots more stations, and they was always on time.'

Ned's starting pay was seven shillings a week and he was general dogsbody for dad and two other keepers. 'I did all the odd jobs such as cleaning and feeding the dogs – retrievers and spaniels – and lookin' after the ferrets. We really kept the rabbits down then. After the main shooting was over I had to get two gallons of paraffin from a shop in the village, soak pieces of sacking, light them and drop 'em down the holes to stink the rabbits out. 'Course you 'ad a lighted piece with you all the time as there was no matches. This took me about a week, then the Guns had a day's shooting and killed about 150 rabbits.

'The keepers always had a nice tweed suit and a cap. We used to go to the best tailor in Wolverhampton – Burslem's, it's gone now. For four guineas you had big, skin leather leggings made in Germany, as well as the suit.

'Shooting was a real pleasure then everybody was happy. I remember one time a Gun's hat blew off and 'e said "Don't worry, my dog will fetch it". Instead of that the dog buried it and we all had a jolly good laugh. It were the sort of thing that made a day. No one was bothered about these huge bags then. If they killed a hundred or more they was really pleased. 'Course, there was plenty of keepers then – everywhere. And there was always plenty of other people to help out on shoot days. We 'ad the lads round at 7am to keep the pheasants in, and later on they'd join in with the beating. In those days duck shooting started on 1 August and we always had plenty of partridges for 1 September.

'In my young days all the shooting was walkin' the fields with the Guns in line through the roots. Partridges were everywhere and there were lots of hares. But it could be dangerous and if you got your dog lost that was the end of it till 'e was found. But I like duck shooting best of all, at night on a fed pond.

'When I was sixteen I took a chap's beat and became underkeeper, with full responsibility for a 140-acre wood at Penkridge. Altogether we reared about 2,500 pheasants and there were traps all over the place then. The hedgehog was the worst vermin on a partridge beat. We 'ad to 'ave pole traps for the brown owl – they was very destructive, but I did protect the white owl.

'We bought some eggs, but plenty was picked up along the roadsides. Then the roads was just rough stones rolled in and when a car went by you saw the dust for hell of a while after.'

In January 1915 Ned joined the 8th South Staffordshire Regiment, 17th Division. 'We went to Lichfield Barracks for five days, then they put sixty of us on the trains and sent us down to Bovington Camp in Dorset. There we 'ad lots of bayonet practice and route marchin' round Tolpuddle and all about. But I took it all in me stride – we

went to serve king and country and thought it'd all be over by Christmas. I met some very decent people, *very* decent, and in England the food was good.'

After two months Ned was sent to Lulworth Cove, where the men were under canvas. 'In April they ordered us to bathe in the sea, but it was too damn cold and we very soon put our clothes on. A month later we marched to Winchester, to Flower Down Camp, to fire our course over the range.' There certainly wasn't much regard for human dignity in the Army then, as Ned bitterly recalls. 'Outside Winchester we all had to line up naked for a medical along the roadside. Anybody could 'ave come along and seen us.

'By golly there were some mugs with rifles there, but we got by. After a short time we got on the train at Basingstoke and went to Dover, then crossed to Boulogne. They took us up in cattle trucks to St Omer and then we had to march

the rest of the way, to a place called St Eloi. We were there seventeen days – went in spick and span and came out lousy as the Devil – just holdin' the line. We had a very good officer for our platoon, S. R. Edwards from Sussex, a grand chap who had the men's interest at heart. He wanted me to be a sniper, which I didn't want. Anyway, he didn't last ten days in the trenches as a shell killed him by my side – 'ad his head half cut right off.

'Then I took up stretcher-bearing and as Lance-Corporal I 'ad eight men under me. This lasted for two and a half years until the regiment was broken up with losses. I was then transferred to the 7th South Staffordshire Regiment, 11th Division. We travelled most parts of the line. It was all bad and dangerous and we got down ready for the Somme advance.

'In July 1916 we started at a place called Fricourt village, where we were rushed after another regiment had been in and got cut up badly. We hadn't been in the trenches long when I heard a shout for help, in no man's land. It was a German officer with a fractured femur, but he was not bleeding. I got some more stretcher-bearers across and we took him to the doctors' dug-out. We always treated everybody the same. Then he pulled his platinum ring off and gave it to me. Since then I have passed the ring on to my granddaughter.

'We then went to Delville Wood to hold on to it after the South Africans had been carved up. I was told there was a man in front wounded, so I crawled forward in the daylight to help him. I was about fifty yards out in no man's land and calling as quietly as I could when I felt a crack on my back. It was a sniper cut my webbing belt off with a bullet. Anyway I couldn't find the man and thought he had been shot so I crawled back into the trenches.

'Next day I had another lucky escape when a shell killed two men in the trench within three yards of me. But everyone had that risk. We wrapped 'em up in oil cloth and took 'em down to the road for collection, but they were still just layin' there a week after when we came away. Your groundsheet was your coffin then.

After two years of marriage it appeared that Alice ruled the Turvey roost!

'I spent my 21st birthday on the Somme, at Hebetune. Mother sent me a chicken and a plum puddin' and four of us ate it all that night. By golly that were a good change. All we had to drink was the water brought up in petrol cans, but the food helped us forget the thousands of rats, which 'ad many a carcass there.

'When I finished stretcher-bearing I was made the sergeant of a platoon, towards the end of the war. And when the big push came it was all over. I happened to be home on leave when armistice was declared. My sister got married at exactly the same time – 11am on 11 November 1918 – at Penkridge church, and I was best man. Then I was transferred back to France and eventually returned to England and Hatherton Hall in February 1919. Then I really 'ad to start work.'

While Ned had been away his father had suffered two serious illnesses, 'So the place was run down, well poached with ferrets and whippets and overrun with vermin. But I soon got busy and gave the poachers and pests a tannin', which is not done today! For each case proved I 'ad 3/6d off the magistrates' clerk – it all came out of costs, so the poachers paid. And if one man had a gun they 'ad the others for aidin' and abettin'. 'Course, the police were different then – great big chaps too.

'I always 'ad a damn good staff [stick] and most of the time the poachers 'ad only got to see it. But sometimes I 'ad a battle royal. Some gypsies came in once – they'd been drinkin'. I sent my son to tell 'em to go, but they didn't so I went up. There were three vans of 'em. I said, "Come on, off you go". Then one struck at me and I 'it 'im with me truncheon on the head and the blood really fled. But I was sorry for him. Then another came on, but I 'ad 'im too and then they cleared off.

'There were a tremendous amount of gypsies about in them days. You were supposed to get the police in to move 'em on. As well as game they took wood for pegs and even ferns to sell. To help catch the poachers we used to set a stuffed cock pheasant by the road and watch for them to come for it.'

In 1931 two of the shooting syndicate died and Ned's father retired. Ned took over as headkeeper for a new syndicate. 'Me pay went up from about 35 bob to £2 a week, rent and rates were free and I had a ton of coal and a suit of clothes a year. The Guns liked about 1,000 pheasants reared each season and there was a good supply of partridges about.'

When World War II came along Ned was exempt from service as he was in charge of a small acreage and required to keep the vermin down and grow crops. 'In any case there was no way I was goin' in that bloody lot again! Feeding the birds was not allowed then but sometimes I 'ad the puggins [tail-end corn] to keep the pheasants together.'

The winter of 1940–41 was very hard. 'The snow blocked us in for six weeks. That's what we're short of now – there's never any snow water to fill the passages up. We only 'ad a small skitterin' this last time [winter 1991–2]. Not like 1947 – that were a damn bad 'un. In the April we went down to Ilfracombe for a while so that Alice could rest after a serious illness, and there was sheep lyin' dead all over the place.'

Family holidays have always been by train as Ned has never owned a car. 'One of the gents was goin' to give me one once, but 'e died. It were tough for the toffs too when taxation got in and then they weren't so liberal. In the old days you always 'ad yer £5 Christmas Box on Boxing Day and that were somethin' then. Sometimes

Ned at home, with a shooting print behind him

people did 'ave a golden sovereign, but never once did I 'ave a £5 tip, not like today when a tenner is looked down on.'

After 1940 no rearing was done, the woods were cut down and Ned worked for various shooting tenants on his own up to retirement in 1962, by which time he had served the 3,500-acre estate for fifty-four years – his entire working life apart from war service. By coincidence, he was headkeeper for exactly the same length of time as his father – thirty-one seasons, 'though I did help out for another month or so until they found someone to replace me.' But sadly, Ned does not have the CLA long-service award for which he is more than qualified. 'I could 'ave gone up to Scotland and 'ad the silver medal *and* a bar, but it were too costly. Anyway, I've got three medals from the first war.'

Having enjoyed thirty-one years' retirement from the age of sixty-seven, Ned remains in very good spirits despite his belief that, 'all your friends desert you when you're old. In the old days people looked after one another. Leave stuff outside now and it'll be pinched pretty quick.'

Ned lives alone now in a quiet lane at Calf Heath, near Wolverhampton, in the house he bought in 1963 ('I sold a few fowls to pay for it'). Proudly, he declares, 'I've never shifted a five-mile in me whole life, apart from time in the Army'. Alice has been in a home for a few years, but Ned has three caring daughters and a 'lad' of sixty-three who works as a ranger. 'I took care 'e never 'ad anythin' to do with keeperin'. It's not like it used to be.

'Today the vermin's doin' untold damage. 'Course, it were a lot easier in my day when all sorts of traps and poisons such as strychnine were still legal. But there

was never any anti trouble and we always patrolled the ground properly so that nobody ever got onto it. And you 'ad to be a very good Shot. When it came to foxes I picked the vulnerable place every time.

'We used to have the hounds over but the huntsman knew what we were about all right. When 'e came by 'e used to call out, "Wiry day today then Ned!" because we kept a vixen and cubs in a wire pen and just let one or two out on hunt days. This were the South Staffordshire hounds, but in the end they 'ad to go because they cut the wire and trampled fences too much.

'Another thing that's wrong now is these damn hoppers. They want to feed broadcast in the wood – make the birds work for it.'

But while Ned laments many changes in keepering he is certainly not a bitter man: he takes a keen interest in everything around him and still writes in a fine hand. His main regret is that he cannot get out into the garden which kept him so active until the last few years. 'They told me I wouldn't last a six-month when I retired, but I took up mole poisonin', and I'd always do a day's beating when I could. Now this sherry's the finest thing to keep me going.' God bless you Ned – the whole of the civilised world owes you a great debt.

Very sadly, Ned Turvey died in February 1993, while this book was in production.

ALMOST A FIXTURE

ALLAN CAMERON

LANARKSHIRE, MIDLOTHIAN AND FORFARSHIRE (ANGUS)

The only trouble with spending all or most of your working life on one estate is that you tend to get handed down with the fixtures and fittings and no one generation of owners or sportsmen can truly appreciate your total commitment. And never has this been more true than in the case of Allan Cameron, whose service on the Burnside estate, near Forfar, spanned seventy years, from the age of fourteen to eighty-four. No few words of thanks from any individual could ever do justice to this extraordinary devotion to duty, but at least now it is properly recognised for posterity within these pages.

When Allan was born, at Motherwell, Lanarkshire, on 15 February 1908, his father was not a gamekeeper, but he could hardly have come from a more distinguished keepering family. His great-grandfather, grandfather and two uncles had all, in turn, been headkeeper for the Duke of Argyll.

'I was the eldest of five children and father was one of ten. There was very little work in the area, so he had to content himself with driving a horse-drawn cart selling lemonade around Motherwell, where he met mother. But he was always on the lookout for a keeper's job. Eventually his persistence paid off. When I was three he became single-handed gamekeeper for the Barrs, brewers at Harburn, near West Calder, Midlothian, working mostly on grouse moor.

'We lived in a tied cottage and I went to Harburn School to the third standard at ten before moving on to West Calder Higher Grade School. They were very strict there. The head used to come round and peer through the little window in the classroom door. In fact he saw more than the teacher, so you were often pulled out and got the strap.'

While still at school, Allan started to help father on the grouse moor, but did not get any pocket money. The only time he received any reward was when he went beating, for which he received half a crown, and a cold pie and lime juice for lunch. The other beaters were generally the four shepherds employed by the Barrs. 'But when needed, father had to help them too, with the shearing. It was big blackface sheep country.

'I also helped father with keeping the rabbits down. I used to go along and draw their necks, then he just had to gather them up and re-set the snares. The ground was just movin' with rabbits then.'

During World War I Allan's father was away in the Royal Garrison Artillery. 'He was one of Lord Kitchener's men and went to the Somme, where his hand was injured by shrapnel and they had to stitch his fingers back on again. From 1916 to 1919 mother took us away from the very lonely house we had at Harburn to stay with grandmother at Motherwell. Times were very hard then and I used to queue for hours at the shops for a quarter pound of margarine, sometimes only to find that it was all gone when it was my turn.'

In 1919 Allan's father returned to his job at Harburn and the family rejoined him there. 'From then on he 'ad to spend six months of the year helpin' the shepherds and he didn't like it. Our lighting was paraffin lamps and our heating was mainly peat cut from the moor. The turfs were stacked in fours – on their ends to dry – and I had to put them up the bank to be carried away, often by mother. Then they were stored in an open shed. We also gathered a little wood.'

As for meals, 'Well, there was always porridge, soup and rabbits, and we got our milk from one of the estate shepherds. The grocer came out once a week in his horse-van, bringing paraffin and other things from the nearest village – West Calder, about four miles away. At Christmas our only treat was a net stocking with an orange and apple in. There was not the money then! Father's wages was only a guinea a week – one golden guinea. There were plenty of them and golden sovereigns at that time.'

In those days there was a lot more game at Harburn. For example, Allan recalls seeing a flock of over 150 black grouse there. 'They're canny birds and always used to fly back over the beaters, so father would give 'em a shot or two to help send them over the Guns. The big lots usually started to gather in November.

'It was just a family shoot there, with lots of rough grass but very few partridges and only the odd pheasant. Grouse was the main thing, and there was plenty of vermin to control. I helped with the heather burning too, and I remember some of the fires gettin' well away, but not with father – he was pretty careful. It was the shepherds who let 'em go. Once one set a whole hill on fire and he was away to his bed. I always remember that, because next mornin' the chauffeur was out gatherin' the abandoned curlews' and other eggs for the big house. Officially, burnin' was allowed up to 20 April then.

'For his shepherding father had to keep a collie at Harburn. He also had Irish setters and a team of pointers. For the first two or three shoots of the season they always walked the grouse. Later on, when the birds were a wee bit wilder us boys were brought in for the driving – always on a Saturday so there was enough people.

'One of my jobs was to feed the dogs – mostly on porridge, none of these fancy biscuits. There was a great big potful boiled up outside. This kept 'em goin' for two days. We also gave them rabbits and cracklin' – a big block of dried beef you hacked pieces off.

Foxes were always high on Allan's 'hit list'

'The collie was also used to hunt foxes in Rabbit Wood, which was in two sections. I used to go in with the dog and drive the foxes out across the gap between the two lots of trees, where father waited to shoot them.'

But despite his early experience, Allan did not go straight into keepering when he left school at the age of fourteen. For a few months he worked for Edinburgh Corporation, who had market gardens at West Calder. There he earned 7/6d a day, 'pulling berries – mostly gooseberries, blackcurrants and redcurrants, and later on all sorts of vegetables.

'Then father got a job as keeper/overseer for Widow Robertson at Burnside, just outside Forfar. At the same time I was taken on as keeper's assistant, in November 1922. I was to remain there for the rest of my working life, single-handed after father died. I'd just as soon 'ave been a gardener but, although there were four on the estate, there were no vacancies at the time. They had six greenhouses and grew everythin' from peaches to melons, but now it's all rack and ruin.

'Everybody helped one another in those days. For example, when the big garden was dug we all 'ad to come in and help for the day – even the chauffeur. And when the hedges were cut we all joined in. That took seven of us two and a half days using ordinary hand shears. Our field hedges and fences always had a yard of cover either side for the game. There was an agreement with the farmers for this. Now the scientists call these conservation headlands and are trying to get everyone on it, but it's nothing new, only forgotten.'

The 1,000-acre Burnside estate then had four mixed arable farms. 'It was all horses of course – one farm had eight. And they always took on extra men at harvest. There were lots of partridges about, but now they are all gone. I blame

the price paid for 'em now – £4 for a young bird this last season [1991–2]. This encourages the lads to creep up behind the walls and poach 'em. Also last winter the dealers were payin' £2.50 for a woodcock and £3 for a brown hare, so it's no wonder they're disappearing. But the pheasants were only bringing £3 a brace, or less.'

As Allan's father had wide-ranging responsibilities at Burnside he was paid a good wage – £3 a week. 'He also had a free house, light, milk and five loads of coal a year. And these were wagon loads too – sometimes 30cwt or more – drawn by horse from Forfar station. Sometimes the estate bought a whole lot from the mine because the other houses had some too. As part of their agreement, the farmers had to do three days a year free carting for the estate.

'At first I was paid £1 a week and my work was all on rabbits. The hill was nearly bare as the road with 'em. Twice a week the chauffeur took the snared rabbits to Stewart's fish shop in Forfar. But in hot weather, when they wouldn't keep, I had to cycle down with them over my handlebars every night when I came in from work. All the heads were tied together so that they didn't go into the spokes of the front wheel, but I still wasted a few bikes with rabbits. I ruined a Rudge in eighteen months. I used to 'ave so many on it I could hardly pedal – even with my legs wide apart. You could get any amount of rabbits then.

'As well as helping with general jobs on the estate, I also used to go out with father to get game for a hamper, which was regularly sent to the family at 2 Douglas Gardens, Edinburgh, or to their London home. A typical lot would include two pair rabbits, two brace pheasants, a woodcock or two, and always several wild duck, as well as occasional grouse.

'We were one of the estates with the shooting on Rescobie Loch. Duck shooting started on 1 August then and every second year we had the first day of the season, alternating with another estate. It was mostly mallard and teal, with a few shovellers, and a big lot of wigeon in winter. The estate had three boats and it was mostly the chauffeur and head gardener went out with father and me. We also used to flight the wigeon – thousands of 'em – at the top of Burnside Hill. Every night they took exactly the same line out to the flooded fields and we always got them quarter of an hour after the mallard finished flighting. We also hunted the reeds out with the dogs, but that was a sore job!'

After the Camerons had been at Burnside for three years, the estate was bought by the Maitland family. 'Mr Ramsay Maitland came from the Woodbank Estate, Loch Lomond. He was a nice gentleman who got his Sir when his brother died.

'That first year he came – 1925 – there was a good stock of game, but we shot so many we had to start rearing in 1926. We always had two-day shoots, starting 8/9 November. The first day would be on the hill, but there were only a few grouse. It was mostly pheasants and quite a few woodcock – we 'ad nineteen twice.

'When we started rearing we caught-up some birds, but there were only a few wild ones about so we also bought 500 eggs from Gaybird and 250 from Westmorland. We had about sixty to seventy hens – I liked Rhode Island Red or Light Sussex best as they were good sitters – and set about eighteen to twenty eggs under each. Every morning I had to lift them all off for feeding, watering and cleaning. We fed them with Indian corn [whole maize].

'Like everybody else at the time, we mixed the chick food. For the first ten days we chopped the usual hardboiled eggs – but only the yolks, though I'm not sure why. There was also Gilbertson and Page's fine biscuit meal and a special drying-off meal. Later on we used chopped rabbit meat and rolled it in your hands with the dryin' meal as the birds didn't like anythin' wet. But it was mainly for the separation really. The young pheasant was wrapped up in cotton wool in those days.

'The birds liked perch too. We chopped the fish up just the same after they was boiled, boned and gutted, but you had to pull the spines off. As the birds got bigger they could take great chunks of fish. We had loads from the lake, so it was free food.

'When the birds went to wood they had mostly wheat and kibbled maize. It was very hard work taking the birds out. With a rope round the neck, two of us would carry two coops, each with a hen and sixteen to eighteen chicks in it. A whole day of that back and forth was enough for anyone. We were out at first light and only stopped when we tripped over in the dark.'

In many ways the birds fared better than the keepers and beaters. 'But they did kill a blackfaced sheep for us at each shoot. We had shepherd's pie one day and mutton stew the next.' Meanwhile, the Guns lunched well at the big house, 'where eleven people, including nurses, worked when the children were young'.

Before World War II, 'poachers used to come out on the train from Dundee for the rabbits, but that line's away now. There's not been that many poachers from Forfar and we've generally known who they are. We used to watch quite a bit at night when the moon was up, but I'd not hide if a vehicle came along: I'd still parade

along the road to give 'em some idea that there was someone about. The main thing always was listening and using your eyes. Happily I was never attacked.'

Nightwatching was often very cold work. However, unlike southern keepers, who generally immediately recall 1946–7 or 1962–3, Allan, 'can't really remember a particular winter – there's been an awful lot of bad ones and they're all about the same. Mind you, 1939–40 was tough, when I was down in Lincolnshire on anti-aircraft batteries. There we used a sheet of corrugated iron as a sledge to get rations on.

'Sir Ramsay (Colonel) Maitland was a right military man and when the war started got us all to join the Local Defence Volunteers. At first all we had was shotguns and his big rifle he used to shoot elephants and tigers with in India. Our observation post was on a hillock lookin' down on Lunan Bay, between Montrose and Arbroath, where they thought any invaders would come in. When it was clear you could see the sea glitterin' in the moonlight.

'We used to just turn out when the siren went. Up here we used to 'ave a road block – just barrels filled with stones: it would hardly stop a bullock let alone a tank. But eventually we got organised a bit and had .303 Ross rifles, not that they were very good.

'One day there were three of us on duty and the siren went. It was a bit misty but you could hear the bombers comin' and I was goin' to have a shot with the

Allan Cameron (centre) with the beaters at Burnside in the early 1960s

elephant rifle as one plane was that low. When the engine noise dropped you could hear the wind whistlin' through his struts. But the mist was just too thick and try as I might I could na see him, and he went on to drop two bombs. It was very disappointing. I tell you that dumdum bullet would certainly have made a hole in him. Old Sir Ramsay took that rifle out stalking once and shot a roe deer. It made a hole so big my father gutted the deer through it!'

At the end of 1940 Allan was posted to Normanby Hall, in Lincolnshire, and stayed in that county on Bofors guns up to 1945. 'We were mostly round Scunthorpe defending the steelworks. The Germans knew where they all were as their engineers had been over here putting most of the blast furnaces in.

'The only narrow escape I had was when a plane dropped this Molotov cocktail stuff all about us. If it had been the normal high explosive I wouldn't be here now telling you this. But we did manage to shoot a Heinkel bomber – it came down two miles away. The people there were so delighted they brought us out all kinds of cakes. You'd 'ave thought we'd saved the lives of everyone in Scunthorpe.'

It was during the war, in 1944, that Allan married Georgina, 'an undercook in the big house at Burnside. There always used to be two Christmas parties for the estate workers then. One was for married women and their families and the other one for married men and single staff. Everyone got a present and there was a good turkey meal.'

Shooting continued at Burnside during the war, though on a much-reduced scale, 'because there was only father and the chauffeur left to look after things. When the Poles were in Forfar they planted a wood for us, which became known as Polish Wood. Father always used to say that the best tip he had was one shilling from a Polish officer. And he never had more than £2 from any gentleman before he died in 1960.

'They was mostly all good Shots in the old days. Lord Southesk and Lord Dalhousie were the best I can recall. And when I was beating for keeper Martin at Drumailbo I always remember the pile of dead partridges laying around Prince Philip. But that was one of the great partridge shoots in Angus and they did rear quite a few.'

Of course, there were disappointing days too. 'At Major Fotheringham's once the Guns were supposed to go forward to a wall and we were goin' to drive the partridges to them. So we started off and covey after covey went over the wall, but not a shot was to be heard. The keeper turned to us and said, "That's the drive and we'll take it all in". Afterwards we found out that the Guns were in the wrong place! There was an argument about who was to blame and the keeper was sacked. Mind you, there had been another disagreement before that.'

Sometimes vermin was easier to deal with than people, and when it came to pests few men were more experienced than Allan. 'In the old days the biggest vermin was the small grass weasel, so before we set the coops out we liked the rearing field grazed as short as possible. But by the time we'd finished the grass was way up. Although you couldn't see it, you always knew it was a weasel because you'd see a pheasant jumping up trying to fly. All you could do was wait for a squeak when it got a bird and then blast at the final flutter and hope that the intruder was killed. Even the young weasels could catch the young gamebirds.

'Sparrowhawks were easier to get as they'd nearly always come back to the same coop as long as there were birds there. All you had to do was wait in hiding and shoot them. We used to go round their nests in the woods too. Father used pole traps when they were legal but I never did.

'The kestrel was the worst to get as he'd come in and hover anywhere in the field, so it was hard to ambush. Tawny owls sometimes took the head off a young bird and then we'd trap them in a ginn.'

Allan has never had any trouble with mink, 'but I did suffer through a brood of wild ferrets, at Burnside just when duck shooting had been put back to

1 September. The release pen was by the big house and one day I found dead pheasants all round by the wire. I ran back to the lodge for my gun and waited for ages, but saw nothing. So I lifted out all the dead birds except five, which I set by Fenn traps just outside the pen because I thought it was stoats.

'In the evening, after a day's shoot, I went back and there in the traps were a bitch ferret and two young dog ferrets. I kept the traps set and ended up with ten young ferrets as well as the old bitch. I never did see the old dog ferret there. But about two months later, a good bit away, one of my snared rabbits was broken open, so I set a trap there and caught him, too.

'Now there's hardly any predator control for miles around because all the old estates have been broken up and most of the full-time keepers are gone. This is partly why all the capers [capercaillies] are gone. The worst thing now is so many foxes getting the eggs and young on the ground. There are a lot more badgers to take them too.

'We always used to get capers round here, but once we shot eight hens in a day and that was the ruination of it. It was the first year a syndicate took the shooting and they were only allowed one bird each, but one greedy Gun shot four! He said he couldn't resist them. But when they stopped shooting them altogether you could walk right up to them in the trees, so that didn't help. They became so tame they were vulnerable to poachers and predators.'

Despite so many years' experience, Allan admits that you never stop learning. Even in his last rearing season he was puzzled by predation. 'It was summer 1991 and I had 200 five-week-old poults. On the second morning seventeen were lyin' dead with a bite on top of the head. I thought it was a weasel or rat, so I went home and got a tin of Cymag and gassed all the rabbit holes round about.

'But next morning there was another ten lyin' dead. So I told the boss I'd put the rest in the pen by the big house. The first night I waited right through till I could na see and the only thing I saw was a hedgehog. But he didn't go in the pop-holes so I let him be.

'Two days later some more birds were killed in the same way, so I stayed to watch all day. Just as it was getting dark a hedgehog appeared and went in the pop-hole, so I shot him. I watched a bit more, then went home.

'Next morning there was nothing, so I thought that was the end of it. But two days later there were more birds dead and I shot another hedgehog. That really was the finish of it.

'A lot of people just won't believe that hedgehogs behave in this way, but I've had them attacking fowls before. They went for their rear ends in the coops, where the hens couldn't defend themselves. Afterwards you always had to kill the birds as they were torn and bleeding. The hedgehogs were also very bad with eggs.'

That Allan was able to continue keepering so actively into his 85th year (he stopped altogether on 23 May 1992) was certainly exceptional. Officially he retired at sixty-five and from then on was supposed to be part-time, 'but it continued more or less the same as there was no one else to do it'. Indeed, his loyalty was remarkable given his disability.

Allan first broke his leg at the age of twenty when he rode over some potholes and came off his Coventry Eagle Flying 350 motor cycle. 'There were no steering dampers to save you then when you got a wobble.' Unfortunately for him, neither did they have X-rays in those days so Forfar Infirmary simply, 'propped me up in sandbags for seven or eight weeks and hoped for the best. But it was never set right and two years later I broke it again while walking a turnip field for partridges.' And not surprisingly, when he broke it a third time, in a rabbit hole after World War II, the leg became steadily worse. Now it is very debilitating, with the main bone pressing sideways and down over the ankle.

Despite the weakness, Allan remained, 'motorbike daft. I finished up with a 500 Norton just after the war. Then I bought a little car – a Ford 8. Mine was a year old, but they were only £115 new then.'

Sadly, his troublesome leg has recently prevented him from taking part in his favourite sport – salmon fishing. 'I still go for the trout at Rescobie Loch – I had a 2lb 12oz rainbow just two weeks ago. But I'd rather have one day at the salmon than a week at the trout. Unfortunately I haven't been able to go for three years now [to 1992]. My best fish ever were two of 25lb each on the fly on the South Esk. I used to go with a chap called Mr Irons just after the war, and we cut the banks with a lawnmower so that we did na get snarled up. Mr Irons had the fishing on the Marcus estate.'

In his younger days Allan was a good Shot too, winning notable competitions with an old family gun. 'Grandfather had this William Ford with two sets of

Angling has long been Allan's favourite pastime

barrels, one heavily choked for foxes. When father got it he had a new stock put on by Dickson's of Edinburgh. During the war he loaned it to a shepherd who never cleaned it. Then I had it and shot with it till the day a number four shot came through a hole in the barrel! That was the gun I lifted the Lour Cup with, at the Lour club near Dundee between the wars. I beat a man who would have kept it for good if he'd won it a third time. But he had a lot of whisky in him that time, and that's a thing I don't take.'

Although this is one Scot who does not take Scotch, he is certainly not lacking in spirit. In 1991 he was presented with a special certificate for outstanding service as an elder of Rescobie church for thirty years. Indeed, he remains actively involved with the church and even as we spoke the minister arrived in his car to tell Allan about a forthcoming management committee meeting. But Allan remembers the days when, 'the minister used to visit us all on a pushbike'. Allan, too, used to cycle to church as a lad, 'but one day I never got there when the back wheel came off as I was hurtling downhill'.

Allan's wife died in 1990 and now he lives with one of his three children, having decided to vacate the keeper's house at Burnside, where he could have stayed on.

From the window of aptly named 'Burnside View', on the outskirts of Forfar, he can see the hills over which he walked so many times, and reflect on the contrasting ways of different generations. Apart from the Robertsons, he has served three generations of Maitlands (Sir Ramsay, Sir Alexander, and lastly Sir Richard), and there is no doubting that he liked the old, more gentlemanly and far less commercialised days best. But then, the estate did have to cope with heavy taxation when Sir Alexander died within three years of his father.

Allan Cameron has certainly served Burnside well, as his brother John still does part-time, having been forester there for over fifty-four years. Now there is no keeper in the family, Allan's only son having taken a different path, but there is no doubting that the name Cameron will echo about the hills of Angus for very many years to come.

Recognition of Allan's outstanding service

PUTTING THE QUEEN SECOND

TOM WALTER

BERKSHIRE, BUCKINGHAMSHIRE, WILTSHIRE AND GLOUCESTERSHIRE

When Tom Walter was presented with a long-service medal at the Game Fair in 1989 he was, of course, honoured to receive it from the Queen, but secretly he was much more excited about meeting someone else. That year the fair was held at Stratfield Saye, the home of the Duke of Wellington, enabling Tom to fulfil a very special ambition. All his life he had wanted to meet His Grace, to tell him about his great-grandfather, who had been gamekeeper to the First Duke of Wellington, the hero of Waterloo, serving Stratfield Saye for fifty-six years.

A kind friend had arranged the meeting and for Tom it could not have come quickly enough. But on the day he was last in a line of ten keepers up for awards. 'The Queen said, "That's a long wait Walter, but now you can meet the duke himself", and then he stepped forward.' It was a fitting tribute to a remarkable career.

Christened Thomas Walter ('There's no *s* on the end even though everyone calls me Walters') was born on 18 October 1908, at Hurst, near Reading in Berkshire. Surprisingly, neither Tom's father nor grandfather were keepers before him, but he did have a keepering uncle on the Haineshill Estate.

'Granny had four sons, all in the Scots Fusiliers in the Great War. Two came 'ome and two got killed. Father was a foreman bricklayer at only nineteen – now that's a credit! He could even show you the join where two bricklayers had worked on one house. I could never see any difference. And he was also a wonderful Shot at pigeons.'

Tom's mother did not work. 'She was too busy with me and my six brothers and four sisters. All my sisters are still going, and two of my brothers. None of them were ever keepers.'

When Tom was at Hurst school, 'Just over the 'edge was Elijah J. Hicks, the famous rose grower who used to sweep the board at Chelsea. He was the only man ever 'ad a black rose. I saw it once, but it died with 'im. We used to see 'im in his greenhouse at night studying the plants.'

To earn a bit of pocket money while at school, Tom delivered the *Football Chronicle*, 'on Saturday nights. I got about two bob for taking thirty or forty papers. I picked 'em up from Reading Station, where each lot was rolled up in a cardboard tube. When I took 'em round all the people was waitin' at the gates for you to get the results.'

Tom's earliest memories of shooting are from when he was about twelve. 'We used to go beatin' different places to stand stop. At lunchtime we had lovely salt beef and cheese sandwiches, a bottle of pop and two shillings. The men had five bob.'

He also managed to make a little money from another sport. 'Three of us used

to run a rat and sparrow club, when we were teenagers. We went round with clap-nets, all about the 'edges and the ivy on the buildin's. Our torch mesmerised the birds and they were soon caught. We tore their 'eads off and took 'em to the farmers, along with the rats which we used to get when we lifted up the floors on the poultry farms. The farmers had a competition to see who could get the most and the winner was announced at the flower show. We used to kill 400–500 rats a year and gettin' on for a thousand sparrows. We won all four years we entered – got about £4 for the sparrows and £4 for the rats, between the three of us. That was a lot then.

'Years ago there was sparrows everywhere – it was nothin' to get 300 or more

in the edge of a wheatfield. We used to get dust shot and if you fired into 'em just right you got dozens. Everyone had sparrow pie then. They pulled the legs out and split the breasts for it. These were the only parts worth keeping. But a lot of the time sparrows were fed to the ferrets which we used to get rats.

'Sparrows are lovely sweet birds, not like a lot of 'em such as the robin and all the tits, which are bitter. With starlings you 'ave to pull their 'eads off and then they are all right. We also used to catch birds such as goldfinches and linnets in the clap-nets, but let them go.'

Tom left school at the age of fourteen to work with his father. 'I think the first thing we did together was build a sectional bungalow, mostly working on the

foundations. I always remember this because they had a water diviner to set the well before placing the house.

'In 1925, headkeeper Jim Martin asked me to be his only underkeeper at Bill Hill, near Hurst. My elder brother, who worked in the garden, got twenty-five shillings a week, but I got thirty shillings as I had to work weekends. Mr Martin even arranged with the police for me to carry a gun on the road at seventeen, when it should have been eighteen. The shooting was let to Thomas Haig, the whisky man, and he was my boss – a very nice man. Shooting was much more fun in those days. Give me the old ways – crack a few jokes then on to the next drive. Each season they only shot three or four times for cocks and hens and once for cocks.'

At Bill Hill Tom had no special perks, 'but always on the last drive of the year Mr Haig called me out of the woods and gave me a new ten-shilling note. He also said that I would get a bottle of port from Martin. But one of the best tips I ever had was in the thirties. K. V. Peppiat – the chief cashier of the Bank of England – gave me a brand new pound note. That was a lot then.

'I looked after one half of the Bill Hill shoot. There was a beautiful, steep valley, but they put the M4 right through it and there's only a little bit of my wood left now. We had a few wild partridges, but most of the work was on 500–600 reared pheasants, which was quite a few in those days. There was a lot of work, with broody hens and the coops twenty-five yards apart. We'd cut a bough off a tree and put it at the back of a coop. Then if anythin' came over the hen would go, *brrr brrr*, and the chicks ran for cover under the branch till she said come out again. I much preferred the old system of open-range pheasant rearing, rather than the pen rearing you get today. The broody hens really taught the chicks how to protect themselves and it made better shooting.

'Now it's all crumbs and pellets, but in my early days we cooked up our own feed for the chicks. There were three sizes of biscuit meal – fine, medium and coarse. For the first three or four weeks the chicks had the fine scalded in a pan, mixed with boiled eggs pushed through a sieve, and boiled rice – there was an art in cookin' that. If you pressed it and there was three white spots in the grain that was the time to take it off. If it was too puddiny you 'ad a job to part it. You see the grains looked like maggots and that's what attracted the birds.

'For the older birds in the wood, farmers often used to bring us carcasses and we'd hang 'em up in the trees to get maggots, which would fall out. The pheasants loved scratchin' around for those. 'As the chicks got older they had Dari seed, buckwheat, hempseed, split peas and groats – that's oats with the husks off, chopped up and kibbled. Yes, there was a beautiful variety of food you could buy then.

'We used to 'ave a bit of fun with the Dari. If you covered a hen's eye and pointed the other at one of the white seeds, and then let her go, she'd stay there mesmerised for some time.

'Poor old Jim Martin had a sad end to his career. When he went to Haineshill he showed somebody where a 500lb bomb had dropped durin' the war. He was standing on the edge of the crater and as he turned round he tripped on some bushes and 'is gun went off and shot 'im in the thigh. People tore up shirts best they could to stop the bleeding and rushed him to Reading hospital, but the leg had to come off. He couldn't work after that.'

After three years at Bill Hill, Tom decided it was time, 'to better meself and apply for various jobs. I could 'ave 'ad the job old Charlie South took at Windsor, but I turned it down as there were too many restrictions. You even 'ad to hand your jacket back if you left because of the buttons with the royal insignia on.

'In those days Crufts was the place to get a job. Old Cruft sold dog biscuits and was really interested in keepers. But anyway, I put an advert in the *Gamekeeper* magazine and 'ad a telegram from Parmore,

near Marlow in Buckinghamshire. I went up one Friday. Tell you what, that's my lucky day: wherever I went I got the job.

'So I cycled up through Henley – about sixteen miles – and got there around 2.30 or 3pm. The Honourable Seddon Cripps, Lord Parmore's elder son, interviewed me in his office. He seemed satisfied, but I 'ad to wait for the other keeper to come back from the family's other estate. Meanwhile I went into the kitchen to 'ave tea with the maids and cooks.

'The keeper asked me to start as his second on the Monday, but on Sunday there was about three inches of snow, so I didn't get to Buckinghamshire till about 12 o'clock on me first day. It was a job even to push the bike so I left it halfway. Then I took me case to Skirmett, where the keeper had fixed me up with lodgin's in the council houses.

'The shoot was let to a lovely man – Sir Sydney Sitwell – and there were big plans for it. We 'ad the local carpenter and his son making 250 coops in a barn for us. There were stacks of wood everywhere. The carpenter also fitted out a shepherd's hut with a stove, foldin' table and gauze-fronted larder and I slept in there on the rearing field for four years. But when I was in lodgin's I 'ad to pay twenty-five shillings a week out of thirty-five shillings wages, which was above the agricultural rate in those days.

'At Parmore it always fascinated me why the pheasants stayed at home because it was all beeches – thousands of 'em – with hardly any cover at all. Wherever you got a few stunted little bushes there'd be dozens of birds in there. But we had the land for some wonderful shooting. The M40 cuts through the estate now.

'We 'ad two hermits there. One had 'is hair right down 'is back. He used to get on the bus and people called 'im Jack Frightenem. The other one was called Luxster Jack and 'e came down to the village to get 'is ten-shilling pension and a few groceries each week. He could also catch a rabbit and anythin' to keep 'imself goin'. He made a shack on my beat and the roof was packed with bracken to keep warm. One day the police told me he was dead and they'd had to shoot 'is dog to get at 'im. He was a lovely chap – never hurt anyone.

'Near old Luxster Jack there was a whirly 'ole – one of those springs that bubbles up. If you got a bottle with a cork in and put it out in the middle it would suddenly disappear – oooosh. Nobody knew where it went.

'After lunch we only had one drive and would blank in all the 'angin' [hangers – steep hillside woods] for three-quarters of a mile. This took between an hour and one and a half hours and the nine Guns – five in the first line – shot 300–400 pheasants. We always had a policeman with us on shoot day – 'e was paid of course.'

With such large bags, Tom and his colleagues obviously needed a lot of feed. 'We used to get it by the lorry-load from James and Chamberlain of Hungerford, and the Polish eggs came in crates of 500. I 'ad two boilers for these out in the field.

'Then one day the headkeeper was throwing coconuts at Thame Show and twisted his knee. He told the boss he did it in a rabbit hole, and next shoot 'e sent another keeper in his place, rather than me. The boss said, "Where's Walter?" So I thought – look out for yourself here! It was time to move on. I didn't want to get involved with anyone tellin' lies. I always say tell the truth and you'll never go wrong.'

Tom then applied for a job, 'at Dashwood's place at West Wycombe. But when

I saw the head he was in hell of a stew. He'd put poison in a rabbit for vermin, just where some children walked through the wood to catch a bus. So when one girl dropped dead on the bus he thought she'd taken the rabbit home. But the verdict was heart failure.

'Anyway, the shoot moved to Ramsbury in Wiltshire and they asked me to go down there. It was run by Thomas Forbes, the insurance broker. But my wife – I married Grace in 1932 – had to stop with mother till the house was available.'

Ramsbury was in partridge country and Tom operated the old Euston system. 'I wish they'd do it today, we might get the grey partridges back. The idea was to find nests when the birds started to lay, pick up the eggs and put wooden ones in their place. When a clutch got to eleven I stopped putting the dummies in. I always

Dummy partridge eggs

operated in odd numbers because birds can count in twos! I always 'ad a string of eggs with me. Just cut one off and rub it off a bit. They were made by friends – mostly from beech – and were much cheaper than the bought ones.'

While the real eggs were in Tom's care they were safe from predators and sudden weather changes. 'Twenty or so would be set under a broody hen. Then, when they were chipping at twenty-two days or so I put them back in the wild nests. It was always best to get them away before they double-chipped at twenty-three days because they could hatch under your shirt as you walked round. I've carried as many as sixty chipped eggs next to me chest. I 'ad a belt round me so they couldn't drop down. People say to me didn't they die of cold, but they kept quite warm for a surprisingly long time.

'It's a wonderful thing to watch the partridges. You often 'ad to poke 'em off the nest with a stick and I've 'ad them fly up and knock me cap off before. As they were hatching off, the cock would come and sit by the hen to help dry the chicks off.

'The only thing wrong with the system was I was the only one who knew where all the nests were. So I said to the old headkeeper, "I'd better show you where they all are in case anything happens to me". He said, "How on earth do you find all these nests?" I suppose it's a gift.

'At Ramsbury we 'ad this poacher called Monty Fox – and 'e was crafty too. Well, with the partridges my main job was finished by the end of June, so I asked if I could 'ave a few pheasants in the wood – to amuse me. So I did. But the head said, "What shall we do about Monty?" I said, "Just give him a couple of bob extra on beatin' day – at least if 'e's here you know where he is".'

At the time, Tom used to enjoy longnetting. 'That's the way to sweep the rabbits up. One night we had seventy-five. Only thing was you really 'ad to know your ground. Run into a patch of thistles or something and that soon snags you up. We used to go out three or four times a week. Now no one knows the trade. We could 'ave 200 yards of net pegged out in three and a half minutes. Two men would drive

in – zigzaggin' – and you 'ad to guess a bit as you might be in front of each other in the dark. A chap took our rabbits to London twice a week and we always looked forward to him comin' round because he brought back lots of fruit, from the market.

'One night I heard thump, thump, thump. It was the headkeeper kickin' a fox, but 'e got out. Worst thing to 'ave in a net was an ol' hare – 'e used to thrash about an' squeal an' frighten everythin' off.

'Another time we started to put the net out when all the rabbits came runnin' by before our men came in. I thought we must be in front of another net – and we were. It was Monty's. So we gave 'im half a dozen rabbits and told 'im to go home and pack it in.

'Monty used to walk through a wood and shoot all the birds on the way back after he'd seen where they were, so that he was in and out as quickly as possible. There was this old tin bath by his gate where birds were left for collection, and one day the police was gonna catch 'im. So they got in the shed opposite and waited. Eventually the carrier came by, looked under the bath and out came the police. But there was nothin' there and off they went very disappointed. Half an hour later the carrier's son turned up and then the birds were in place. The thing is, the police shouldn't 'ave blabbed about what they was gonna do.'

In 1936 Forbes warned Tom to start looking for another job because he expected to lose most of his money following a shipping disaster. As a result, through recommendation Tom secured his first single-handed position, for Major Huth at Wansdyke End, Inkpen, near Hungerford. 'He and his wife had two Wolseley cars with numbers one after the other. The shoot was 1,600 acres in one big block, with only a little wood. It was all partridges on top of the downs and a forty-foot-wide sheep drove went all the way to Marlborough.'

After a year the major asked Tom if he could do anything about the moles. He replied, 'Yes, but we'll need a lot of traps. So I got ten dozen. Well, you can only catch moles in quantity from the first week in March to mid-April, so this worked in well with my Euston system.

'The major and me used to listen to this series on the wireless about a professional mole catcher. One day he said to me, "Did you hear the professional caught sixty-five moles in a 19-acre field?" I said, "I can beat that – I've caught ninety-two in four days in a 15-acre field".

'Altogether, in Wiltshire I caught about 4,000 moles in five years. One place I would catch four or five in the same trap in one day. They like a damp path best. Twice I've caught two moles in one trap going in opposite directions at the same time. Later on, in Gloucestershire, I caught twenty-two moles, one weasel and one toad in a trap that was never moved. That was in a grass garden path.

'I used to sell the skins to Friends for a penny or tuppence. Cock pheasant centre-tail feathers fetched a penny each and a lot of chaps used to slip a few out unnoticed on the big shoots. Magpie tails and pairs of wings were worth fourpence each and jays' wings about threepence a pair.'

Tom did not have to go to war. 'When it started the major said to me, "When does your age group come up?" I said, "It can't be long as all my six brothers are in it already". He said, "I'll stop that – it's far too much for one family". And he did, bein' an Army man himself.

'We had a rifle range on the estate – right in the corner of Wiltshire and Berkshire – and I looked after it for the Home Guard. The Americans came there too and we used to get a few sticks of Wrigley's spearmint from them. At the same time I carried on with my Euston system. We had twenty-five old English gamebirds, so there was always plenty of hens.

'There were a lot of interesting guests on the shoot, including the Marquis of Aylesbury from Savernake Forest. He trained fox terriers to find truffles and came over to us with his headkeeper in a chain-driven Trojan car.

'In 1946 the major called me in and asked me to check over his pair of Cogswell & Harrisons, which I always looked after anyway. He told me he was too old to shoot any more and was going to sell the guns back to the makers. He said that if I see another job I should take it, but if I wanted to I could work in the woods.'

That year Tom took a job as single-handed keeper at Adbury Park, near Newbury in Berkshire. 'It was an old family shoot and they didn't care if you only got twenty or thirty a day. I left in 1952 when they was goin' to let the house as a boys' school. I thought, that's no good with boys runnin' all over the place.'

Tom's next stop was Salperton Park, in Gloucestershire, working for the Hulton family – 'the *Picture Post* people. Dr Zezi, a Harley Street man, looked after the shooting. I always remember when I went for interview, it was the day King George VI died. The master at Stroud station told me the news and when I passed it on to the people in the carriage they said rubbish!'

Life at Salperton was quite traumatic for Tom. 'Dangerous! Corr! I remember old man (Sir Edward) Hulton shooting a pheasant on the wall and all the shot came back through me and the beaters. And we had some well-known guests too, including the authors A. G. Street and Macdonald Hastings.

'There was one time Sir Edward was determined to shoot a hare, but we walked all day and he couldn't shoot anythin'. Then I got really fed up, so when 'e fired I fired too and at last we bagged one. He never did know. I didn't want to walk no further.'

After just two years, Tom could not stand Salperton any longer. 'The farm manager didn't like 'untin' and shootin' at all and did everythin' he could to spoil it. He even got a gang of gypsies to camp right by my shoot, when they were supposed to be potato pickin'.'

In 1954 Tom's fortunes changed, when he went to work at Northleach, Gloucestershire, on Colonel Raymond Barrow's Farmington estate. 'He was a proper military man. If 'e said 'e was goin' to pick me up at six it had to be six – not quarter to or quarter past! But he was a lovely man.'

Tom has lived and worked on the Farmington Estate ever since, the first thirty-one years in one house, up to his retirement from full-time work in 1985, when he moved to his present cottage. 'I still look after a little bit of wood, helpin' Captain John Barrow's present keeper.'

Remarkably, Tom has never learned to drive or owned a vehicle, but that has never stopped him carrying out his duties efficiently. He believes that when you drive about you do not really see what is going on in the countryside. Yet, as Captain Barrow says, 'everybody knows him for miles around and he always knows what's going on before everybody else. He is a wonderful character and a real countryman.'

In everything he does, Tom appears to be blessed with a sixth sense. 'I suppose it's a gift. If you're out in the woods waitin' for a stoat, suddenly you know it's there even before you look round.

'One evening I was stood by this chap watchin' the pheasants go to roost when suddenly the whole lot got up and flew to the other end of the wood. He said, "There must be someone in there". But I said, "No, somethin's goin' to happen tonight". And sure enough it did – we had five inches of snow. Nature's a wonderful thing, but if you want to know it properly you've got to live with it all the time.'

Unashamedly superstitious, Tom has had quite a few unnerving experiences in foretelling events, some extremely sad. 'We 'ad a blackbird used to come out 'ere on the wire and whistle away while my wife was unwell up in the bedroom. Then one day as we were going out my daughter said, "What's that black thing on the ground by the gate? Someone must have dropped a glove." But I knew it was the blackbird and told her to go on. I would pick it up. And my wife died that evening.

'That was four years ago and people say to me, "Don't you ever get lonely?" But I say no – I've been lonely all my life in the woods. And here I've got some wonderful neighbours and friends, as well as a son and daughter who visit me. Also, there's the birds on the nuts all the time. I've had over thirty tits at once.

'But I really miss the birdlife there used to be. We don't get half the numbers now. Down in my woods there was always half a dozen chiffchaffs or willow warblers, but now there's hardly one. And back in Berkshire there were lots of nightingales.'

Tom is obviously very knowledgeable when it comes to birds and has been lucky enough to find a few rarities in his time. 'The most unusual was a pair of hoopoes – my father saw them too. Another time, in Gloucestershire, there was a foot of snow in the woods and as I walked through all these bits fell down on me. It was a flock of crossbills feeding in the trees above. And I've only once found the nest

The hoopoe

of a hawfinch. It was halfway up an oak tree on a tuft. You can always tell hawfinches because as they fly along they've got a certain twitter.'

This great knowledge of birdlife has been especially useful to Tom in vermin control. 'I don't believe in traps. Only do it if you've got to. If you happen to get took bad no one but you knows where that trap is. I only used the old pole traps and ginns when they was legal and there was a very bad case, but I never used poisons.

'You can get everythin' you like if you go at the right time. Always remember that birds of a feather flock together. At one place the carrion crows come four miles to roost in a certain wood – way up in the trees. Only snag is it's a long way home in the dark. Anyway, I put this jackdaw on a fishing line and pulled it in a field where the crows used to gather before goin' up to the roost. By golly, didn't they come down to mob it. I got seventeen the first night. A lot of keepers also used to attract crows with a ferret on a line.

'With magpies too the best thing is to walk about and find their roost. They like a patch of bramble in a big wood. Then you want a good wind and shoot 'em. One place I had sixteen in an evening, and I could 'ave got more if I could see in the dark.

'Foxes have never been a big problem. I could call one up anywhere. Once I called two right through my legs! Mating time's always the best because then they've only the one thing on their mind.'

*He was told to
swallow the slug*

Tom, at home, reflecting on the old times

Jackdaws have given Tom a few headaches. 'At Ramsbury they used to get in the pen first thing in the morning and take the pheasants' eggs. One day I was cycling downhill on my way to deal with 'em when a rabbit ran into the spokes of me front wheel and drove the stays of the mudguard up and into my arm as I went over the top. See – I've still got the scars. Mind you, the rabbit came off worse – 'e ended up with a neck a yard long.'

On another occasion Tom was injured by a horse. 'I never liked them much anyway. We were playin' cricket and I went to get the ball when this colt lashed out, split me lip and knocked me senseless.'

But Tom's most serious injury was not at the hands of an animal. 'It was about twelve years ago on the last shoot day that year. I was runnin' through the wood when a bit of nut stick stuck in me eye and snapped off.' At the time Tom did not think too much of it but eventually it caused problems with the sight of both eyes, which he has sometimes lost despite several operations. Today he still has problems focusing and finds it very hard to read.

Fortunately, Tom has never been seriously injured by a poacher, but he has helped to nab a few. 'When I was at Inkpen, the nearby keeper at Fosbury, Ronnie Legg, used to hear a few shots before he went off in the morning. I said, "that must be one of your own people as he seems to know exactly when you're around. You want to go off and then come back unexpectedly." So 'e did, and it turned out to be the estate plumber, who was sacked a couple of days later.

'When I was at Adbury Park I knew keeper Charlie Maber of Highclere – Lord Carnarvon's castle. He said 'e 'ad someone gets a pheasant occasionally but he didn't know who. I said, "Does anyone come up to see you regularly?" He said, "Yes". Turned out it was 'im too. Whenever this man came over to see Charlie 'e stood 'is gun by a tree and bagged a bird on the way back. You've really got to try to out-think some of these people.'

Inevitably, gypsies were involved in many of the poaching incidents in Tom's day, but they also had their uses – as the providers of magical cures. Perhaps the most bizarre Tom ever encountered was during his time in Buckinghamshire. 'This man 'ad this tapeworm which all the experts just couldn't shift. Then a gypsy told 'im that the only way was to go out next time it was raining to get one of those big, black slugs. Then he had to swallow the slug after puttin' it in salt water to get rid of the slime. It worked all right because I saw the tapeworm in the yard. It must have been thirty or thirty-five feet long.'

Throughout all these adventures, Tom has encountered some very severe weather. Not surprisingly, his memories of the bitter winter of 1962–3 remain sharp as Gloucestershire was hard hit. 'One day the colonel said to me, "Let's go and see the snow." So off we went, and there was this coffin stuck in an 'earse. It was there for three weeks. Then there were stranded lorry drivers all over – goodness knows what they did for food.

'The colonel used to ride down on his white horse, Stuffy, to get the village post. And we was forever diggin' people out. Then we got a snow-plough for the village. Nowadays, Derek from the farm gets out with it whenever the snow sets in. But some of these people moan, "What's Derek doin' clatterin' about at night?" So I say to them you weren't 'ere in '63. If you 'ad been you'd soon be glad of it.

'One of the worst times of all was the first year of the last war. Everythin' was froze up – even a piece of grass was wide as a board. If you could run you'd catch the hares, the ice was that thick on their backs. Loads of branches, even whole trees, came down with the weight of ice. The milkman never came for three weeks. When I managed to get my shed door open I left it open as I'd never do it again. I went to help the shepherd get 'is sheep and when 'e dropped 'is stick it shot downhill at a terrific rate. And when the sheep was down to the hay you 'ad to watch out – they'd be on top of you they was so hungry. All the rabbit holes were almost frozen right over and the rabbits lived off the chalk – their mouths and teeth were all white.'

Today all these intriguing observations of wildlife form but one tiny part of the vast nature encyclopaedia in Tom Walter's memory. Few people have known the outdoors so intimately or served their masters so well. Even his great-grandfather would be hard-pressed to match such a record.

BIG BROTHER
WALTER WALLER

YORKSHIRE

The incredibly agile 84-year-old Walter Waller is a remarkable man from a remarkable family. Not only has he been the backbone of a friendly farmers' shoot for some sixty years, but also he has enlisted the help of brothers George (83), Jack (79) and 'baby' Bert (77) as beaters. Surely their combined service of 232 years at one place – the Todwick shoot, near Worksop – and aggregate age of 323 must constitute some sort of shooting record?

Though small in stature and quietly spoken, Walter's authority and leadership are unquestioned. While lesser men flounder over the sodden winter plough, he strides across the skyline with all the grit for which Yorkshiremen are famed. No one would dream that he is a lifelong asthma sufferer, and even when the M1 motorway sliced his precious patch in two he remained undaunted.

Such devotion to shooting is unusual for a man not from a long line of keepers. However, he does come from an old farming family who seem to have been on the land since before the gun was invented, and in Yorkshire at least farming and fieldsports have always gone hand in hand.

Walter was born on 16 March 1909 at Aston, near Sheffield, where his father and grandfather ran a small mixed farm. 'We 'ad a bit of everythin' in them days – cows, pigs, the lot. And it were the best partridge shoot around, sandwiched

The four Waller brothers: (left to right) Jack, George, Walter and Bert

between two big, keepered estates.

'Fred Brown was the first keeper I ever knew. He worked for the Verells on the Aston Hall estate. When I were just seven I remember seein' 'is vermin pole in Nicker Wood and I 'ad to 'ave one. That wood's nearly all gone now.

'In the same year I had my first shot ever and I shall never forget it. I used grandad's single-barrel 12-bore. He made this hide and a pigeon came in, but I didn't hold the gun tight on me shoulder like 'e told me, so over I went on me back. The pigeon was sittin' but I still managed to miss it, even though grandad bothered to make me a rest for the gun as I was so small.'

It was as a schoolboy that Walter became accustomed to walking long distances. 'We often used to trudge the six miles to Rotherham market or the eight miles to Worksop.' This was ideal training for a lad whose heart was set on becoming a keeper. Indeed, this was Walter's goal throughout the time he was at Todwick School.

'During holidays and weekends I used to assist Tate, the keeper at Aston after Brown. I helped with the feeding and release of both pheasants and partridges, all reared under bantams. I used to get ants' eggs and soften wheat in water for the young chicks. We also mixed hardboiled egg yolks with ground wheat.'

But like so many country lads at the time, Walter was so preoccupied with fieldsports he was often late for school or tempted to 'skive off'. Inevitably, the day came when he was caught out. 'Mrs Verell was a keen hunter and the Grove hounds [now the Grove and Rufford] often met at Aston Hall. One school lunch-time me and two others went down this little cart road and hounds came past. We got under this 'edge and some of the horses jumped right over us – never knew we were there. But we were late back and as we ran up the road we met the old carter who growled, "Miss Barwell's waitin' for you with the cane".

'Another time, again when I was just seven, I was watchin' the hunt at Aston and I'd never seen a fox. I said to myself, "I wish a fox would come across here", and to my astonishment it did. Up came the huntsman and asked, "Have you seen the fox?", and, with a broad grin, I was able to tell 'im where it went.

'I also got into trouble with the school attendance officer through stayin' home to help father on the farm. But when I was 14 I started with 'im full-time, helpin'

Some of the horses jumped right over us

with the thrashin'. There were two thrashers – steam-driven at first, and a corn carrier with riddles which sorted the grain, even the weed seeds, into three grades. The wheat was put into enormous eighteen-stone bags; barley, sixteen stone and oats, twelve stone. Yet there was little chaps runnin' about carryin' them no problem. They got six shillings a day in the twenties, and even into the thirties, which was one of the worst times for agriculture and when thousands of acres went wild.

'But even then it was all changin' so fast. As a lad, me grandfather rode what we called a putting-off machine, and as he went he raked the corn in. As soon as he 'ad enough he pressed his foot down and put off a sheaf. Two lads made the bands and two men took the sheaves away.

'There were also two big orchards and a huge greenhouse for tomatoes, and I can remember seein' thirty women pickin' raspberries. Great Uncle used to go to Sheffield market Tuesday and Saturday, settin' off at 2am with his horse and dray. He was one of three brothers who worked the farm with grandad.

'The game was all wild on our 80-acre farm, but the magpies and weasels were very bad so the main thing was vermin control. In the early 1930s I asked some neighbouring farmers if I could shoot over their land and some of them joined in the sport. About six of us just walked around, mainly after pheasants, partridges, wild duck, snipe and woodcock.'

But these were tough times and it was not long before the farm had to be sold. It was bought by a nephew. This prompted Walter to spend more time on keepering, so he was delighted when Lord Marchwood of Todwick Grange sent for him. 'I hear you're keen on looking after game and vermin', he said. It was an opportunity not to miss.

Hardwick Grange.
Aston
Nr. Sheffield.

I have known Walter Waller
all his life, & have every
confidence in recommending
him for a gamekeeper.
He is a young man of sound
character, honest & sober, and
of very good connections.
Keep on Vermin etc, but had no
pheasant rearing experience here.
I am sure under right guidance
& your help, he will prove a success.

Yours faithfully,

Thomas. Curtis.

Letters of recommendation
and thanks

MANOR HOUSE,
CHOLDERTON,
Nᴿ SALISBURY.

CHOLDERTON 200.

13th May, 1958.

TO _WHOM _IT _MAY _CONCERN

I have known Walter Waller for some
twenty years now. During the war and after
it he acted as a part-time Keeper for me on
a Partridge Shoot in South Yorkshire, working
all hours virtually for the sheer love of
it and producing excellent results.

He has gained his experience the
practical way and I feel would make an
excellent Keeper.

Viscount Marchwood

Headquarters,

Western Command.

2 Jan 45.

My dee Waller.

I do congratulate you on the simply excellent day
we had last Sunday week.   It could not have been more
perfect and I personally enjoyed every minute of it.
Perhaps because I shot better than I have done for some time!!

Please let me know what the final bag was after
the "pick-up", as I feel that if we had had more dogs we would
have had something like 25 brace.

Don't forget to let Mrs. Penny know about the Beer
for the Farmer's Day and also let me know how it goes and
what you get.

Do you think it would be too late to arrange
another drive for the week-end of the 27th January, or would
most of the birds have paired by then?   I feel that with
some guns who would be prepared to leave obvious "pairs" alone
it could do no harm, but would like your views.

If you agree I will try and get Major Machell, Mr.
Neil Peech, Mr. Jim Peech and possibly my father and either
Mr. Cyril or Mr. Hubert Nicholson.   All this on the basis that
I can get leave myself!

I wrote to Mr. Hartley to thank him and also to
Miss Wright who says that we can shoot her land at any time
both sides of the road and right up to the house, providing
we mention it to her beforehand.

With all good wishes to you and Mrs. Waller for the
New Year.

Sincerely Yours

Mr. Walter Waller,
Goosecar Lane,
Todwick,
Nr. SHEFFIELD.

'Lord Marchwood shot only six days in the season as he was in the Army. It was all wild birds on his 800 acres so again it was just vermin control required. But there was always plenty of game. I remember one Saturday mornin' it rained like all that and 'is lordship said to come at three o'clock. There was just three Guns but they shot 39½ brace grey partridges in only two hours. Now all the hedges have been pulled out and it's no good at all.

'At first Lord Marchwood used to come to shoot in a little ol' Austin 7, but one day after the war he and Lady Marchwood arrived in a Rolls Royce. I said, "Has the boat landed sir?" and he said, "Yes – the Japs had to pay me compensation for my business". They were a marvellous couple, and I taught their son to shoot.'

Walter looked after the Marchwood shoot – virtually for nothing – for the ten years to 1949. 'I didn't do much else as I was an asthma sufferer and failed the Army medical. But I did join the fire service when the Germans was bombin' Sheffield. I was livin' in Todwick village and rows of bombs was dropped all round here. But it was a bit like *Dad's Army* really, all we had was a hand-pump so we didn't go to any big fires, and luckily there was none in the village.'

When the Marchwood estate was sold and split up it was bought by various farmers and Walter continued to look after the shooting for some of them. Again the pay was token, but Walter was untiring in his efforts and persuaded other farmers to join, eventually embracing 3,000 acres from Anston to Treeton. 'In those days there were little 20-acre fields and lovely hedges up on banks ideal for partridges. Now, so much of the cover has gone, but we still shoot on about 1,500 acres across eight farms. Also, the present farmers are makin' a real effort to help the game and wildlife.'

Walter's patch has always been primarily partridge country, and for many generations it was simply a case of keeping the vermin down to let them thrive. But a number of things changed this, especially development of the mines and the fug of air pollution from many coke ovens around Sheffield, which killed or

PHILIP MURPHY

retarded so many hedges. This was not surprising when even a barbed wire fence disintegrated in only about five years and the curtains in farmhouses rotted rapidly, in the acidic atmosphere.

Fortunately the air is a lot cleaner now and surviving hedges are recovering, especially with the encouragement of shooting farmers. However, the closure of so many pits has left a lot of men out of work and aggravated Walter's poaching problems. 'They've all got whippets and are out here at night when we're in bed. Only last week we 'ad the lamp men in, at two o'clock in the morning. There's an awful lot of night shootin' round 'ere. As soon as the harvest is over the lamp men start comin' after the hares, with their big, powerful lamps shinin' straight into the houses. Some people phone the police they're so alarmed, but all they say is, there's no point us comin' as they'll be gone when we get there. Well, I can remember the day when a bobby was as interested as you are.

'There used to be 300 people in the parish, now there's 2,000. They all come out of the towns and think they can go anywhere. They tell us we ought to 'ave more sense than shootin'. Some of 'em have even been on to the council to stop us shootin'. Now all the old cart roads have been turned into official footpaths or bridleways, but all my life they was only for farmers – the council's got no idea. We get people up 'ere all the time trainin' for greyhound racin' at Sheffield, and they soon turn 'em loose if you're not careful. But some are really poachers and you always have to watch it. One man even threatened to shoot me if I came any nearer.'

Another major blow came in the mid-1960s, when the new M1 motorway split the shoot in two, creating much disturbance and spoiling many drives as well as taking precious land. Now, almost everywhere in the area, the atmosphere is spoiled by the day-long drone of traffic. Along the A57 at Todwick it has become so bad that Walter has had to install double glazing and the view from his window is spoiled by creeping suburbia. 'It were marvellous 'ere for songbirds in the old days. Mind you, it's not so bad now – I fed my robin just before you came. And the other night I 'eard an owl I 'adn't 'eard for years. This man 'ere comes out from the town and the other night 'e said 'e 'eard someone squealin'. I said "don't be daft, that were a little owl that were!" '

Walter married Alice, now aged eighty-three, in 1933. They have lived in Todwick for over forty years, about half that time in their present house, which belonged to their only son, an art teacher who died of cancer. Sadly, their only daughter also died young, of pneumonia, so the longevity and health of the Waller brothers is all the more remarkable. In fact, Walter is one of nine children. Apart from the four brothers in the shoot, 'who all still have their own teeth', claims one

Walter (right) is saluted by his 'baby' brother George (Dick), an 82-year-old beater

of the Guns, there are twin sisters of sixty-seven and a sister of eighty-seven. 'One of my two dead brothers was killed by a lorry. Father died at eighty-three and grandfather at ninety-seven, so there might be a few miles in me yet.'

They have had many a tough winter up there too. 'In 1947 the snow on the A57 was level with the walls through the village. Although the partridges was all wild they really relied on you then. The cold came after a good game year and the birds were waitin' for me when I went round in the snow, puttin' the feed of lightly crushed wheat along by the sheep-netting. That lot didn't start till the last week in January, and a farmer friend 'ad only just said to me, "Aren't we gettin' the winter over nicely". It lasted for weeks and weeks and there was snow down by that 'edge there well into June.'

On Walter's shoot the emphasis remains very much on the social side and variety rather than big bags. With the brothers at the centre of things, there is none of the division between Guns and beaters which rather spoils some pretentious shoots. It is very much a family affair, with Wallers beating, shooting, picking-up, keepering and laying on that splendid Yorkshire hospitality – usually starting with a warming drink in the farmhouse kitchen of Walter's cousin Bert, as Guns draw for pegs. Outside in the cold, the land is under siege from mounting economic pressures, but the character of these people is as strong as ever. Fools are not suffered gladly, but not every man here is as outspoken as the *Yorkshire Post*. Some lead chiefly through sheer enthusiasm and example – none more so than the irrepressible Walter Waller.

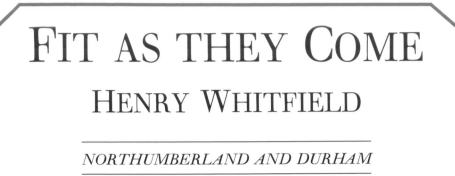

FIT AS THEY COME

HENRY WHITFIELD

NORTHUMBERLAND AND DURHAM

As the decades roll by, most elderly keepers must move down a gear, often going part-time if allowed to stay on. Few continue full-time into their eighties, and even fewer do so with *two* shooting syndicates to look after. But that is exactly what Henry Anthony Whitfield has done. Furthermore, he has a grouse moor as well as low ground, enough to tax the average man in his prime. Yet Henry remains the picture of health and contentment. But perhaps that has something to do with the fact that, after a long absence, he was lucky enough to return to the unspoilt countryside where he was born and grew up, as well as the benefit of all that invigorating fresh air.

Henry's remarkable achievement and standing in the community were obvious when over 200 Guns, beaters, keepers, farmers, foresters and other guests attended his 80th birthday party, organised in 1992 by the two syndicates he has served so well. It was held in a marquee at 'the big house' and Henry was given some splendid presents, including a beautifully mounted grouse – 'for me the only gamebird'.

Back in the late 1960s and early 1970s, Henry already had such a great store of knowledge he was invited to write the regular high-ground keepers' column in *Shooting Times*. His popular pieces, under the pen-name Henry Farnham, ran for five years and complemented the telling words of legendary keeper Harry Grass, who wrote on lowground topics. But Henry was not one of those scribes whose wide-ranging expertise was acquired overnight. Indeed, it was the product of a long, hard apprenticeship to the outdoors, which began in the early years of George V's reign.

One of two children, Henry was born on 22 August 1912, 'about a mile up the moor' from his present home, the delightfully situated old schoolhouse, in the hamlet of Hepple, Northumberland. At the time his father was in his third year as gamekeeper on Sir Walter Buchanan-Riddle's Whitefield estate, having previously been underkeeper at Roddam, a little to the north. His grandfather, too, worked at Whitefield, being head gardener in charge of six staff. 'Grandad had a tame fox that walked about the garden with him. He put it in the toolshed each night, but come the mating season it was away.'

From the age of five, Henry attended the school right next to the house where he now lives. Sadly it is now closed, but between the wars it was a thriving seat of rustic education. 'Every day the teacher used to put the attendances on a slate above the fireplace, and the highest I can remember was fifty-four. That was a lot for here, but the kids used to walk from a radius of two and a half miles and there were mostly large families and many more people on the land then. It was a complete community in every way and the village had its own blacksmith and priest.'

But one thing that has not changed greatly round about Hepple, unlike in most

of the country, is the wildlife. Henry assures me that the birds and flowers remain 'much the same as they were' in this delightful corner of Northumberland. 'There's been hardly any building here either, so we are very lucky. In the old days at home we had the usual oil lamps and it was always upstairs to bed with a candle. The only time we ever went away was on the annual school charabanc trip, but we were happy then.'

Henry certainly had plenty of opportunity to cultivate outdoor interests. 'I hung on to father's plus-fours wherever he went', so it was not surprising that young Whitfield always wanted to be a keeper.

'I was five when I took my first shot – at a post. Father stood behind me and held my shoulders. His guns were supplied by the estate. Much later, in 1938, I bought a Henry Atkin double hammerless gun for £8, from Armstrong's in Northumberland St, Newcastle. It was thirty or forty years old then and I still have it, so it can't be long to its 100th birthday.'

From the age of twelve, Henry started beating on his father's grouse moor. 'There were about twenty to twenty-two of us, much the same as today, but whereas we got 6d a day they now get £15. There were more children then, but otherwise it was mostly farmhands. We always had the main shoots on Saturdays as that was best for beaters. Men were given a beer and us boys lemonade.'

Although Henry continued to help his father with vermin control, when he left school at 14 he did not become a gamekeeper immediately. In fact, rabbit catching was to provide his main income for the next seven years. 'I joined a lad who already had a business. The countryside was alive with rabbits and we'd either give the farmer a price – say £100 or £150 – or get paid about 6d a couple caught. You had to judge carefully which was your best bet.

'We used snares, traps and ferrets but we always left sufficient rabbits to breed. There was no myxomatosis then and it was a good living. The dealers came out once a week in a van from Newcastle. We ran about 300 snares each and it was heavy work putting them all out, gathering the catch and re-setting on a different field two or three times a week. Then there were the holes to dig to bury the guts.

'The bulk of the grouse on our estate went to the gamedealer, too. But some went into the house as well as to the Guns. We had an ice house there and the birds were stored in there as well as in the wine cellar. I can remember seeing maggots drop out of the grouse onto the concrete floor, and that's when they started to eat them.

'Sir Walter was a great Shot and over the years had all the bigwigs over, including Lord Montgomery. He wouldn't shoot with more than six Guns and never shot more than eighty brace. We've had over the hundred brace a few times since, but there aren't the good Shots there used to be.

'Lunches were good too, in an old hut built on the peat. The butler and the woodman took the food, table-cloth, silver and all, out in panniers on a horse. Very often, when they arrived back at the hall they were staggering about where they'd drained all the empties. Father also had a pipe into a nearby spring so that he could take a jug of spring water to the Guns' whiskies.'

At the age of sixteen Henry became interested in his father's bees. 'One day a bee chased me out of the garden and into the house. Then I was determined to

Henry Whitfield at 22, in his first under-keeper's position

A well-earned rest: the Ray estate headkeeper at the grouse butts in the late 1930s

conquer them, and I did. It's been my hobby ever since.' Indeed, Henry has enjoyed great success as a beekeeper. In the 1950s he won the London national competition for heather honey three times.

'The last time I showed in London I took the thistle honey and won first prize among sixty to a hundred entries in the dark class. I used to put the honey on the train in special travelling boxes for shows all over the country, but I stopped when the local station closed down.'

Today Henry has some twenty hives and is a member of the Alnwick branch of the Northumberland Beekeepers' Association, for which he sometimes gives talks. As far as bees are concerned, he describes where he lives as, 'a hungry district, with the bees working up to about three miles from the hive. They usually start the year on sycamore. Then, if the weather is suitable, move on to hawthorn, followed by the main crops from clover and heather. But in 1992 there's been masses of thistles and it's years since I've had honey like this.'

Soon after Henry became keen on honey, he also fell for another sweetness. At the age of nineteen he met his future wife, Evelyn. 'She worked in the baker's at Rothbury and we had a lovely time going round to all the dances where they did the catering. Rothbury had a railway station then.'

Three years later, at the age of twenty-two, Henry was 'called on to be underkeeper for the 10,000-acre Ray estate, owned by Parsons, the engineers, near Otterburn, about ten miles away. There was only the headkeeper and me, and my wages were £2, but there was no uniform supplied. They could shoot three days a week, with bags of 100 brace of grouse, and not cover the same ground twice.

Blackcocks displaying at lek

'Ray had its own private railway station and there was one train a day to Kielder. The line terminated at Morpeth. This meant we could send hampers of grouse by rail. But you had to keep watch every time the train came through the estate as the sparks from the old steam engine would set fire to the heather. But you didn't have to wait there long because, if it caught, the smoke would come up as soon as the train went past.'

However, deliberate, rotational heather burning is essential for good grouse management, to provide a succession of nutritious shoots on which the grouse feed, as well as cover of a suitable height for birds to nest in and hide from predators. 'There's always plenty to burn', says Henry, 'you can never keep up with it. The shepherds have always been the worst burners because they're not bothered about grouse and don't control the fires properly. We had one fire up here at Hepple that went for two days and burned down three fences. These shepherds just go away and have their teas and forget

Feeding time: Henry on the rearing field at the Hermitage in 1937

about the flames. But nowadays it can be very dangerous with all the new forestry around.

'It was the forestry that destroyed much of the blackgame habitat. Black grouse used to be all over Northumberland. I had thirty-two at a lek once. A chap wanted to photograph them and I told him to come out at 3.30am to get in the right position undetected, but it was 7.15am before he got that wonderful picture there on the wall. Later he tried to photograph a golden plover nesting at Whitefield, but he failed. That's a very cute bird.'

After three years on the Ray estate, Henry was again 'called upon' and went to work as underkeeper for Sir Arthur Wood at the Hermitage, Chester-le-Street, Durham. He was obviously keen to get some experience with pheasants because the move meant a drop in pay to thirty shillings. His new headkeeper, Wigmore, was from Henry's area.

'It was a private shoot of only about six or seven hundred acres, but we shot about the 200 mark. It was hard going, feeding the birds four times a day, at 7am, 11am, 4pm and 7pm, and I was in a bothy with six gardeners, but Sir Arthur was a good boss.'

Chester-le-Street was in a much more heavily populated area than Henry had been used to, so the risk of poaching was far greater. 'The first thing they handed me was a policeman's truncheon. I always carried it, but my beat was quite remote and luckily I never needed to use it.'

In 1939 Henry and Evelyn were married, 'but Wood couldn't fit us up with a house. I think he thought he'd have to pay me more money if he had done. But anyway, Wigmore fitted me up with a job at nearby Lambton Park, where I got thirty-five shillings a week and was quite happy. We got all our coal too and sometimes the fire was never out for a week.'

Another perk for Henry at Lambton was 6d per head vermin money, paid weekly. 'You had to keep the heads or tails to get this and it was mostly for rats and winged vermin. But what took my eye was the number of jays there. I knew

they liked maize so I put a handful on a small platform I made to go on the side of a tree. The maize was next to the tree and I put a trap on the platform where the birds would land. I had an awful lot of them. The headkeeper said to me, "Where did you get all these?" He was quite beat by it as there were no Northumberland chaps down there. But at least he learned something.

'The late Lord Lambton was a brilliant Shot, just as his son is now. There was a superb drive over the river, which was in a deep gully, and then another one back. All the while there was a keeper and another man in a boat below to gather up the birds which fell into the water. Altogether there were six of us on four beats at Lambton, plus a lad with a pony and cart who did nothing but supply us beatkeepers with food for the birds.

'But I never thought I'd stay down there on the pheasants. I always expected to go back to the grouse. And then the war came along and in a way Hitler did me a good turn. But I never dreamed I would eventually end up going back to the estate where I was born.

'Anyway, the shooting at Lambton had to wind down. All the pheasants were in the woods in September 1939, at the start of the war, so we shot them to the end of the season. Then all of us, except the headkeeper, were paid off and left in February 1940. Evelyn and I got the bus home from Newcastle to Rothbury and took our spaniel with us. We didn't want to leave anything behind.'

For the first few weeks the Whitfields stayed with Evelyn's mother. Then Henry 'got back into Whitefield, helping father with anything. But my brother on the estate had already been called up, so I volunteered quickly to get the choice of trade – motor transport.

'I had a great life in the RAF, but once you're in uniform you want to get out of it. Anyway, I trained at Arbroath, square bashin', then went to Blackpool to learn to drive, even though I already knew how!

'Eventually 4,000 of us left Liverpool docks on a troop ship and halfway to America we had a buzz up with a sub. Then we turned south and east and ended up at Bombay. We were never told where we were actually going, but we had the Far East kit issued before we left, so we had a pretty good idea.

'From Bombay we spent a week on the train getting to Calcutta, and then we went ninety miles north to a remote hill station called Salbani. After a while I was called up to the office and I thought I was in trouble again with my letters, which were always heavily censored. And I'd devised a code to tell Evelyn where I was, by making words up from the first letter of each sentence. Perhaps they'd discovered my secret.

'But I was only partly right. The officer said, "First, be careful with your mail. Second, don't you recognise me?" Turned out we'd met back in Northumberland and there we were in the middle of nowhere halfway round the world. It was just before I left home and a Spitfire piloted by a Free French lad crashed on our hill. The shepherd told me and I told the police, who informed the services. A gang came out and I showed them the plane. The officer in charge was the man now ticking me off in Salbani!

'After that we hung about Calcutta a bit, Hitler's effort finished and we planned to invade Sumatra. But we didn't get there because while we were still at sea the

Yanks dropped the atom bomb on the Japs and we diverted to Singapore.'

Not surprisingly, the Whitefield shoot was fairly run down when Henry returned. 'Father had stayed on but he'd lost interest a bit and the heather was out of control with no burning. But I was delighted to be back. You were thinking about home all the time you were away.'

At this time there was still only grouse shooting on the estate, but interest in pheasants was to develop when the shoot was let. Sir Walter was tragically killed on the estate when his horse put a foot in a rabbit hole and he was thrown and broke his neck. 'His son John was only six months old when he took the title, so

The goshawk – on the increase

the moor was then let to Sir Charles Trevelyan of Cambo, Northumberland. He had it as a family shoot, but they did a lot of walking up and that killed the moor. They only wanted the exercise really.

'Then the Pumphrey family took it, followed by Guy Renwick for eight years. After that the present syndicate led by Peter Vaughan took over. Now there are six Guns, but they always have two guests and shoot eight butts. Mr Vaughan also runs the pheasant shoot, but with a different team of Guns. Altogether we have some 5,000 acres. Sir John doesn't shoot much at all. He was the Prince of Wales' private secretary for five years and now he's away a lot in banking.'

But no matter who is shooting, they only get good sport because they have a good keeper. And one thing Henry is particularly hot on is keeping on top of the pests. 'It's a never-ending job and there's no doubt I do more killing over the boundary than I do within it, especially on the Forestry Commission land. But they like it because I keep an eye on things while I'm over there.

'We've had mink up the river for about ten years now. And I'm certain it's the mink that cleans the young otters up. That's the reason why there's hardly any left in Northumberland.'

Henry has also been very concerned about the return of the goshawk, which has been making a strong comeback in northern England through afforestation as well as escapes and releases. 'It's the main bird of prey here now. But I think the two worst on grouse generally are the hen harrier and the kestrel, especially the kestrel.

'Once I was watching a brood of grouse over the boundary while we were having a bite at midday. A kestrel came and took the whole lot, one by one, back to its nest. Another time, at the Hermitage, a kestrel kept returning to the same coop until it had taken all the young pheasants there. Kestrels are especially bad where a railway runs through a moor and they have plenty of poles to watch from.'

Crows are a perennial problem of course. On Henry's patch they are almost entirely carrions. 'We've only had a few hoodies down from Scotland in very bad weather. But the carrions mysteriously flock up in late winter.'

As I spoke to Henry, a jet fighter flew over his house very low and noisily, as they often do in that part of Northumberland. 'Don't they upset the grouse and sheep?' I asked. 'Never', he replied. 'It's only certain people gets upset by the planes and all the Army manoeuvres, but they're all quiet just now as it looks as if our boys have got to go off and fight for them again!' He was referring to a proposed peace-keeping mission to Iraq and possible UN intervention in Yugoslavia.

Fortunately, Henry's shoot is not an Army training ground, but he still needs to keep his wits about him at all times. All grouse moors are potentially dangerous places, as Henry knows only too well from an experience at Blanchland, in Durham. 'I was flanking and the nearest person to Captain Parlour in the end butt, about 150 yards away. It's always a dangerous place to be in. Anyway, I was very low down and a grouse came through very low between us. He fired at it and a few pellets hit me in the face. He was a tremendous game Shot and I wasn't going to say anything. However, his men told him what had happened and he came over to apologise. He said, "I'm sorry, but the only thing I've got here to cure that is this", and with that he pulled out his flask. By the end of the day I was feeling much better! But a couple of days later two pellets oozed out of my cheek.'

There have been occasions, too, when Henry has needed to help others in

Honeyed existence! Henry has
kept bees since he was 16

distress on the moor, especially as it is such a popular area with ramblers. 'A few
years ago, on a Sunday morning, I saw a group of old people going up a right of
way in cold weather. Then they suddenly stopped on the skyline and I could see
something white on the ground. So I went up in the Toyota and it turned out that
one lady had suffered a heart attack. I fetched the ambulance and a week later, when
she'd recovered, I was sent a bottle of whisky and a thank you letter.

'The moor can be a tough place for the elderly. Even the shepherds come further
and further down the hill the older they get. Eventually they end up in the town,
and there's so many of them on part of a council estate in Rothbury it's known
as "The Shepherds' Rest".

'The worst winter I can remember was the famous one of 1962–3. We were cut
off for weeks, but we didn't have the snow blower then. There was also a year in
the seventies when we were cut off for a week. When you get a storm like that I
like a good wind with it so that the heather bares a bit quicker and the grouse can
get to it.'

For getting about the shoot, Henry favours a Land-Rover. 'I started with them
just after the war and still think they're the best, though expensive compared with
other makes. In the days before the war everyone used to congregate at the hall
and it was all walk, walk. It's hard to understand – now it's all vehicles but we don't
seem to take in any more ground.'

But despite the very considerable aid of modern off-road vehicles, the moor
keeper still has a lot of walking to do. That Henry continues to cope with it so
well is surprising considering a couple of accidents he has had. 'I've snapped the
main tendons in the front of both legs. The first one went when my knee buckled

under me on the stairs here, and the physiotherapist told me I'd never walk the hill again. Second time round was when I slipped into a drain on the moor. Luckily there were two keepers with me or else I'd still be there now. After that the physio said, "This'll definitely floor you", but it didn't.

'I have no intention of retiring. It's been a wonderful life being involved with nature. I'm still learning and I'd do it all again. We both would – we've had some very happy times together.'

Much of the Whitfields' pleasure has come from their working dogs. No less than eight of them lie buried in their garden, 'some in the front, some in the back and marked by headstones. They're all in proper coffins too – we've got a carpenter next door. But you have to start digging after dark or else you might worry people a bit. It was always an awful thing when a dog died.'

But at least one of Henry's dogs had a very lucky escape. 'In the 1950s our terrier Vic was missing for twenty-one days after a hunting expedition and we'd given up hoping. Then one day he came trotting back home, all bitten and his head bigger than his body. We can only imagine that he was stuck in a fox hole and eventually scrambled out when he was thin enough.'

The Whitfields have also known some great two-legged characters, such as the roadster who called himself Richard Overhead. 'He was an old Army regular who just turned up from nowhere and lived down the road in a dilapidated Pele tower – one of many built across northern England for the people to retreat into when the Scots came down on their raids. He had a box and came round once a month selling needles, pins, cottons and other things. But there were only about fifteen calls, so I can't imagine he made much of a living from it. Still, he was a canny old devil. Evelyn and mother used to carry food down to him when he became ill.'

There is no doubt that anyone unlucky enough to be in Richard Overhead's position today would be equally well received in the Whitfield household. Rarely have I encountered such a contented couple. 'And sometimes I even know when he's coming home from work', says Evelyn, 'because from the window I can see the beaters' flags on the last drive of the day.'

A Life on Two Wheels

Fred Bayfield

SUFFOLK, NORFOLK, KENT, HAMPSHIRE AND SUSSEX

Eighty-year-old Fred Bayfield is one of the real old-school gamekeepers who have never owned a car. Indeed, he spent his entire working life on two wheels, persisting with pedal power until he retired from full-time keepering at the age of seventy. Only then did he accept the relative luxury of a moped, for a further ten years' part-time work. His record is all the more remarkable for the fact that he smoked for most of his life.

But then, Fred truly was born to the task, coming from one of the most distinguished keepering families during the heyday of gameshooting. Christened Frederick John Bayfield, he was born on 19 October 1912, at the Elveden estate,

Fred's headkeeper grandfather (left) with his underkeeper (right) and other staff on the Earsham Hall estate in 1886

Pictured in 1880, Fred Bayfield's great-grandfather, John, who was headkeeper at Earsham Hall, Norfolk

Earsham estate hatching yard in 1902

Fred Bayfield's father, beatkeeper at Elveden,
in 1910

on the northern boundary of Suffolk. At the time, his father was a beatkeeper on
the Guinness family's celebrated shoot, later becoming headkeeper at Earsham
Hall, Norfolk, a position also held by Fred's grandfather, great-grandfather and
brother. Three of Fred's other brothers became keepers too. One was headkeeper
at the Easton estate, near Norwich, another headkeeper for brewer John Cobbold
at Little Glemham, near Saxmundham, and a third became beatkeeper at King's
Walden, Hertfordshire. Today the family tradition continues as one of Fred's
nephews took over from his father as headkeeper at Little Glemham.

One of nine children, Fred went to Elveden school from the age of five. 'Most
of the sixty or so children there were from the estate, as Elveden had a huge acreage
and many workers. There were twenty-four keepers, a dog trainer and about eight
warreners apart from all the farm staff.

'During World War I father was in the Machine Gun Corps and went to France and Russia. When he came back he was given a beat at Eriswell, on another part of the estate, where he took over all the rearing of the pheasants. He also became loader to Lord Iveagh and travelled all over the country with him.

'When we moved I went to Eriswell school, from the age of about eight. Then I 'ad about two miles to walk – in all winds and weathers. Our two teachers were very strict and no one dreamed of skiving off. I enjoyed school, especially the nature walks, but that learning was bred in us.'

Even though Elveden was always a very progressive estate, workers' cottages in those days were as basic there as in most other places. The brick-and-flint Bayfield home had the usual outside toilet and a well, and was lit by paraffin lamps and candles. 'Father also had a free ton of coal a year and the old tin bath came out for a scrub in front of the fire on Friday nights. But we did have one modern convenience. All the Elveden keepers were connected by phone to the estate office. It was run by battery and you took the earphone off the wall while you spoke into the fixed apparatus.' The estate also had telephone post sockets into which portable instruments could be plugged.

One of the highlights of the year at Elveden was the workers' party at the end of harvest. 'It was held in marquees near the big house, but the families at Eriswell were about six miles away so the women and children were taken on horse-drawn wagons with tarpaulins over while the men went on their bikes. All the horses were done up in their brasses and special ribbons for the day. A lunch was provided for the men and they were still drinkin' the beer when their families arrived for tea. There was sandwiches, sausage rolls, ginger beer, games, racing and the local brass band. And I can remember everyone singin', "For he's a jolly good fellow" at the end of the day.

RETURN OF THE SHOOTING AT ELVEDEN.
6th 7th 8th November 1923

DATE.	BEAT.	GUNS. see back.	PHEASANTS.	PARTRIDGES.	GROUSE.	HARES.	RABBITS.	WOODCOCK.	VARIOUS.	TOTAL.
6th	Sugarloaf.	5	911	835		97	37	1	13	1,894
7th	Chamberlain's Buildings	6	814	770		85	32		7	1,708
8th	Napthens & High Lodge	6	790	312		88	39	2	6	1,237
	TOTAL		2,515	1,917		270	108	3	26	4,839

GUNS.

H. M. The King

The Duke of Leeds

The Earl of Mount Edgcumbe *

The Earl of Albemarle ×

Capt Sir Bryan G. Faussett.

The Hon Sir Henry Stonor.

Capt Hon Alex Hardinge +

* 6th 7th, × 8th, 7th 8th, Nov, 1923.

Elveden,

6th 7th 8th November, 1923.

Elveden game card for 6–8 November, 1923, when the King was one of the Guns

'Just before Christmas, Lady Iveagh would come round to each house with presents for the children. I remember getting a pair of short trousers. We never got silly things like toys. I expect they asked our parents what was needed. Otherwise, all we used to get in our Christmas stocking was just a few sweets, a piece of cake, an orange and apple – anythin' cheap you could get hold of then. That was mother's job to fill it up.

'Another real highlight at Eriswell was when the headkeeper Tom Turner came over. If father wasn't around he took me for a ride in his pony and trap to find him.

'A further treat came in 1921, when there was a terrific drought and our well dried up. We 'ad to 'ave water brought to us from the river and father had to take water round to the wild English partridges. It was put in Gilbertson and Page self-filling drinkers, which would usually fill up with the rain, and even a little from the dew. Father had a seventeen-gallon milk churn full of water, but as he needed to take it round in a wheelbarrow he wanted me to carry his gun in case he saw any vermin. That was a real highlight for me, even though I was not yet allowed to have a shot.'

With such a constant clampdown on vermin it is not surprising that Fred can never remember seeing a magpie at Elveden. 'But there were plenty of red squirrels and sparrowhawks.

'The shooting was excellent and we always had a lot of partridges. One day Lord Iveagh consulted my father and they decided to drive the partridges into the wind on his beat. Then Lord Albemarle from nearby Quidenham, whose family owned Elveden a long time before, said to Lord Iveagh, "In no way will those partridges face the wind". But Lord Iveagh insisted he wanted it done that way. Anyway, the drive turned out to be a great success and afterwards Lord Iveagh said to Lord Albemarle, "I ask my guests here to shoot, not to plan the shoot".'

Two years later, Fred's father became headkeeper at Earsham, owned by Major Meade, who let the shoot and hall to Cecil Oliverson. Fred was ten when the family moved into a large cottage on the estate, which was near Bungay, south-east of Norwich. Unfortunately for him, the teachers at his new school were as severe as those at Eriswell. It made no difference that the headmaster had previously taught his father. 'He was a very strict man with a frock-coat and a cane hidden in it.'

This house, too, had a well in the garden. Fred clearly remembers that it took 'exactly forty-seven turns on the wheel, one of us on each side, to get the water up, and the bucket contained ten gallons so it was pretty heavy. That was bootiful water, but when they was goin' to modernise the cottage in the 1970s they tested the water and said it was unfit for human consumption, even though mother had brought up nine children on it!'

The family ate rather well at Earsham. Although there was the usual abundance of rabbit pies and stews common to most keepering households at the time, they had regular treats too. 'It was always roast beef and baked potatoes on Saturdays and cold on Sundays. Now most people have the joint on Sunday and cold on Monday, but my brother still does it how we used to. I don't know why we did it that way round.

'Another thing, there was always porridge for breakfast and mother baked her

Gamekeepers all: young Fred (centre) with his father (left) and brother Rupert (right)

own bread twice a week. Also, there was plenty of fish with a fishmonger in the village. It was collected daily from Lowestoft, which was the nearest port, and when herrings were in season you got about twenty for a shilling.

'We lived about a mile out of the village so we mostly had to make our own entertainment. But this was quite easy with a large family and we used to play a lot of cricket and football. There was a big ol' walnut tree just outside and us boys used to spend a lot of time knockin' the nuts down, but we heard later that it got blown down in the 1987 hurricane.

'All of us went to church and Sunday school and sung in the village choir at Earsham. I liked that. Mother was very religious and used to read to us out of the Bible and sing hymns to us when we were young. My parents, grandmother and great-grandparents are all buried in Earsham village churchyard.'

The only occasion when Fred received some pocket money was when the funfair came to Bungay. 'Father gave me and my brothers 6d each, but we had to weed the garden path first.'

However, he did regularly help father with the rearing. In fact, when he was twelve, he liked it so much he asked to have his own birds. 'I had twelve coops of pheasants in a wood and had to feed them early in the morning. Then I went back home for breakfast and after that, on my way to school, I carried a can of water down to the pheasants. I brought the empty can back on the way 'ome to dinner later on. Meanwhile, father fed and watered the birds for me midday.

'I was still not allowed to have a gun, though I had been taught to shoot with a single-barrel .410. I still remember my first shot. I caught this baby rabbit and took it to father on the rearing field. He said, "Do you want a shot at it?" So 'e cocked the gun, I snapped me eyes, expecting a big explosion, pulled the trigger and – click! He'd deliberately left the cartridge out to see my reaction. But then he put one in and I fired. It seemed like an almighty jar on my shoulder, but at least I hit the rabbit.

'Later on that summer holiday father was havin' trouble with a litter of stoats on the pheasants. He took me down the woods with a double-barrel .410 and four cartridges and told me to put only one cartridge in the left-hand barrel, and I was to sit and wait on my own. But nothing happened and it got a bit boring, so for devilment I put two cartridges in and cocked both triggers. Then I was playin' about and one barrel went off. Father soon came back and asked me what I'd shot. I had to tell him the truth, so then I was sent home in disgrace and told I was not to use the gun again for another month. That was a good lesson that was.'

Thus it was not surprising that Fred never wanted to do anything else other than keepering. Fortunately for him, there was a place available under his father when he was old enough to start work. 'I was fourteen in the October, left school at Christmas and started as boy keeper on 1 January. Most of it was cleanin' out the ferrets and dogs and acting as rearing-field boy. Unusually, at Earsham they did not shut the pheasants up at night, because there was a keeper watchin' night and day. But I never did that because I was too young.

'But we did a lot of ferreting then – every other day at the end of the shootin' season – and I liked that. All five underkeepers helped father and on ferretin' days I was sent down to the pub, The Duke, to fetch their beer. They had a gallon of Steward and Patterson mild at 4d a pint. I collected it in a stone jar which I carried in a side feed-bag, along with two half-pint earthenware mugs, which they had to share. I was allowed a little. This was a daily ritual when rabbitin', but if it was very cold they made do with half a gallon of old beer, which was very dark and used to warm 'em up. In those days there were three pubs in the village but now there's only the Queen's Head left. They also took out their half a cottage loaf and cheese each for lunch. But they never stopped work for long.

'The rabbits were generally bolted and shot because the burrows were mostly

too big to net and the more you walk about on top of them the less the rabbits will bolt. These burrows needed four Guns and a dozen muzzled ferrets.

'We stood and shot at each for about an hour and when it all went quiet we put the guns down and brought in the line ferrets – left, right and middle of the burrow. These were not muzzled so that they'd get right up to the backed-up rabbits and kill them. The muzzled ferrets would keep scratchin' the back of a rabbit where it couldn't kill it, and when you got it out the rabbit had a bare patch on its back. The liners were mostly dog ferrets and drove the loose ferrets – mostly does – back out. Then you 'ad to dig.

'The line on the ferret was knotted to length so that you knew how far in it was. We also used the Norfolk spade with a long spoon-shaped end and a long handle with a hook on it. The old craftsman used to stick this in and listen through the handle for the ferret scratchin' about below. When he was right above it he knew where to dig down. Some people put their ear to the ground. If the ferret was in too far you could use the hook on the spade to get the line, as well as hook the rabbit out when you were close enough.'

Catching rabbits in quantity was heavy work. 'The recognised rule was that you never put the loose ferrets in after three in the afternoon. Legend was that the rabbits wouldn't bolt after that. But the days were short then anyway, in January, February and March, and after you gathered all the rabbits up there was still the paunching and burying the guts. It was always my job to dig the hole!

'We usually got sixty or seventy rabbits a day and they all had to be manhandled back to the larder. If there were many more I used to fetch the cart, pulled by a donkey. He was a stubborn devil. If I got up in the cart to ride he'd stop and I'd have to get out and lead him. Goin' home was different though. Then he used to go at a gallop, even with a full load.'

The rabbits were collected twice a week by a dealer from Loddon. 'For some reason he always paid in cash with a damn great wad of notes. Rabbits fetched good money, but it all went to the estate. Us keepers didn't get anythin' – it was just part of our work.'

Fred's starting pay was 12/6d a week, of which he had to give ten shillings to mother. 'That only left me half a crown spending so I had to be careful. I started smoking at fourteen but had to go for the cheapest cigarettes. Woodbines were five for 2d the same price as Smith's crisps in the blue packet and Player's were 11½d for twenty.

'A really special treat was Saturday evening at the local picture house in Bungay, watchin' the silent movies with someone playin' the piano on the side. It was mostly Charlie Chaplin films and cost 4d to go in. There was a man stood outside with a hessian bag of peanuts, which he measured out in a half-pint mug for 2d. Everybody used to take 'em into the cinema to eat and throw the shells on the floor.'

In addition to his pay, Fred received one suit of clothes a year. 'It was £7 for a three-piece plus brown leather leggings. But you had to buy your own boots. We always 'ad horsehide with a zinc plate in the front – 18/6d from Hogg's of Fife. But they used to last a long time if you looked after 'em properly and kept 'em oiled with Mars oil, which had a brush on the lid when you unscrewed it.

Guns on the Earsham estate in 1927

'You had to buy your own wellingtons too. The first pair I ever had were Bullseye, black with an arrow on and made by Hood's at eighteen shillings. But you couldn't wear them on a shoot day – that wasn't allowed.

'It was all mail order then. Keepers used to get catalogues with all the products in during early August, before the season started. But there was none of this, "allow twenty-eight days for delivery" then. You just sent off your postal order and got the goods back by return of post.

'To help pay for our winter boots we caught moles and skinned stoats and sent jays' wings to Horace Friend. There was also vermin money – penny for rats and twopence for everythin' else, such as hawks, owls, jays and magpies, though there were very few magpies. It was always surprising how many hawks and owls there were considerin' the number of keepers around.'

At Earsham, and so many other estates at the time, rats were 'the biggest problem'. A much less intensive system of agriculture, with lots of hedgerows and corn stacks in the stackyards, allowed them to proliferate. 'We used to poison 'em with arsenic, which the headkeeper bought in bulk from the chemist. We fed them twice for two days on barley meal, then missed a day to make them really hungry. On the fourth day we went round with a 7lb calico bag containing barley flour which the headkeeper had mixed with caster sugar and the arsenic. It was placed well into each hole using a spoon on a long stick. Each underkeeper did his own beat. We also used to put strychnine in eggs and rabbits, mostly for crows, but that was allowed then.'

Earsham was a private shoot. 'They usually shot for three days, Tuesday to

Thursday, then had a break for two or three weeks while the gentlemen was away shootin' other estates. But they always shot continuous for the last ten days of the season. On average days the bag was about 700 and they always bought a lot of eggs to make up the stock.'

The one Gun who stands out in Fred's memory is a Mr Davidson. 'After the last drive of the morning he used to line all the beaters up and march them back to lunch while he played the mouth-organ.

'Lunch was taken in one of the keepers' cottages. One day, as usual, father made out the game card at the end of the morning and gave it to the butler, who passed it to the boss so that he could see how we were doing. Well, this morning we'd already killed 700 and the boss said it was far too many. "There won't be enough left for another day", he declared. So he told father to pay off half the beaters and decided that we'd go down on the marsh and do some walkin'-up to fill out the day. In those days the beaters were paid five shillings, loaders ten shillings and pickers-up 7/6d.'

Although Fred was surrounded by family and friends at Earsham, inevitably the time came when he wanted to spread his wings. In any case, he needed to gain wider experience. But it was a very sad day when, as the eldest son, he flew the nest at the tender age of sixteen.

'I saw this advert in the *Gamekeeper* magazine, for boy assistant at Bearsted, near Maidstone in Kent, and father wrote off for me. I was accepted without interview. When the day came for me to go, father took me down to Liverpool Street Station, across London, and put me on the train at Victoria. My belongings had been sent in advance, in a tin trunk on the train for one shilling.

'It wasn't too bad goin', but when I got to the other end I was really homesick. The headkeeper, who immediately struck me as a very smart man, met me and took me to lodge with him. But his family had grown up and left home so I found it pretty quiet. My wages were twenty-eight shillings and lodgin's eighteen shillings so he just gave me a ten shilling note each week. There was no uniform supplied.

'We were right at the foot of the downs and they looked like mountains to me comin' from Norfolk. It was my first taste of a syndicate on the Thurnham Court estate. There was only the headkeeper and me, but it was a bit easier than back at home because there everyone had put on me, and this was a much smaller shoot.'

However, there was one thing that Fred did not like in his new lodgings. 'I was not allowed to smoke indoors. But I got on well with an ex-keeper who was a gardener and he used to come up most nights to help. He taught me to roll cigarettes, which was good to economise, and that's what I did from then on. I used Hearts of Oak tobacco, which cost 8d an ounce, and AG papers, which were a penny a packet, but not like the interleaved ones you get now. You 'ad to blow on 'em to part them and they was always gettin' stuck together in the wet.'

Once a fortnight Fred wrote home to mother and she wrote back with family news. He did not get any tips, but at Christmas he was able to tell mum that the headkeeper had asked him if he would like a half sovereign or a ten shilling note. He chose the gold coin and still has it now.

Apart from the fact that he saw his first grey squirrel there, at the end of 1929, Fred did not find work at Thurnham Court specially interesting. So when, after

only one season, general recession caused the shoot to fold, Fred was not sorry to leave. 'They told me about a month beforehand that I would not be needed after January and I departed on 13 February, which meant I had both arrived and left on the thirteenth.

'The headkeeper took me up to Cruft's at Islington Hall, where we met father and he took me back home. At the time Cruft's was the highlight of the keepering year. You could say it was where all the pheasants in England was reared and shot! Everybody used to get drunk as lords because all the dealers were after business and put on free drinks.

'While we were at Cruft's we made a few enquiries for me, but we weren't too worried as a Gun who shot with father was also in a Hampshire syndicate requiring a boy. He would speak for me. And so he did. There was no interview again, but

PHILIP MURPHY. 92

I was only offered the job on a month's trial.'

Fred's new shoot was on Sir Frederick Fitzwygram's estate at Leigh Park, in Hampshire. 'I went by train via Liverpool Street, Waterloo and Havant. Again I lodged with the headkeeper, but this time it was a busy house as he had four children plus two more over the four years I was there. So I was not a bit homesick. There was no vermin money, the lodgings cost me £1 a week and my pay dropped to twenty-five shillings, but there was a suit of clothes a year and after the month's trial I did go up to 27/6d.'

This was a very different shoot for Fred. 'It was mostly pheasants, with a few wild partridges, but there was this massive block of hardwood covering some 2,000 acres – a forest compared with what I was used to. Altogether there were about 3,500 acres and only the two of us, but there was a lot of roughshooting days. Our main days brought bags of about 200, and we had quite a lot of woodcock.

'It was a syndicate of mostly local businessmen and again there were no tips, so you had to rely on catchin' moles and skinnin' stoats for a few bob extra. But for the first time ever I was provided with a lunch on a shoot day. The headkeeper's wife did it for me, as well as all the Guns. I had a happy time there and after a year my pay went up to thirty shillings.'

Unfortunately, the shoot was close to some large centres of population and for the first time Fred was severely troubled by poachers. 'It was awful for that. They was mostly after rabbits and came out from Charlotte Street at Portsmouth, which was dead rough at the time. When the pubs chucked out – 10 o'clock in them days they came out with their longnets.

'These poachers were too strong for us, so we put down short lengths of barbed wire and thorn bushes laid about to snag their nets. But this was not always possible on farmland so we also used to go out about 7.30 in the evening with dogs and drive all the rabbits in. Once driven in they were reluctant to come out again for some time so the poachers couldn't get them.

'I 'ad a bit of a scare one night when we were drivin' the rabbits in. I was walkin' about 100yds out from the wood, in the dark, and the head was about 100yds further still. Suddenly I heard someone come runnin' up behind me and I froze. I turned round and saw this great big feller standin' right close to me. He shouted a bit and asked me what I was up to. But he turned out to be the farmer's son, who was an amateur boxer and doin' the same thing as us. It was quite a relief.

'We never actually got attacked by anyone there, but one mornin' we found some cudgels made from chair-backs left under a tree. They were dead crafty those poachers and always came when there was a wind so that the rabbits couldn't hear 'em.'

Nineteen-year-old Fred at Leigh Park, Hampshire

One bright spot at Leigh Park was when Fred met his future wife, Freda. 'It was towards the end of my time there and her father was the estate woodman, but we didn't actually go out together then.'

Eventually the syndicate folded and Fred was given a year's notice. 'I was only back home for a week or two when the Gamekeepers' Association, which you joined for about ten bob a year, told me of a job at Lindfield, near Hayward's Heath, Sussex. I went for interview but I didn't take it because the head wanted me to do a lot of extras such as polish his boots, chop wood and fill the copper up for the Monday wash.

'Then the Association told me of two other jobs – one at Goudhurst, Kent, and one at Stedham Hall, near Midhurst in Sussex. Father knew Major Neave, the secretary of the Gamekeepers' Association, and he recommended Stedham. So off I wrote. The head was a friend of Major Neave, so in the end no interview was required. I was twenty-one and this was my first beatkeeper's job. At last I had some real responsibility. I was over the moon to be able to work on my own initiative.

'Stedham was owned by Mrs Scremouger, who let to her brother, Captain Gregg. There were eight keepers and I got £2 a week plus one suit a year. The head found a family in the village for me to lodge with for £1. The estate also gave me a £10 joint of beef at Christmas. It was a rich syndicate and I started to get tips, which were shared out by the head on 1 February. It was always a great day when he opened the box. The first of the six years I was there I got £7, which was the most money I'd ever had. And after two years my pay was increased to £2 5s. There was no tax but I paid 9d a week national insurance.'

Captain Gregg was well connected and here Fred saw many more distinguished Guns. 'George VI came once when he was Duke of York. They picked out the best day for him, but the bag was about the usual – 700 or so. He shot with 16-bores and didn't seem to be too interested in things. But I suppose he had a lot of invitations.'

Fred recalls that Grimwood was a very strict headkeeper. 'He was old-fashioned – all brown boots and spats – and you 'ad to call him mister. No Christian names in them days. But he was fair.

'It was very hard work there, especially over the nine weeks or so on the rearin' field, working from 6am to nearly midnight at the end, with shuttin' the birds up at night. But every Sunday we did get a quart bottle of beer each. You had to take it to the pub to get it filled up.

'Every week I had to take six rabbits into the house to give to cook for the staff.

Once when I went in she asked me if I would skin and paunch a hare as Olive the kitchen maid was on holiday. So I obliged and she said, "After you've washed your hands I've got something for you." Then she handed me a paper bag and off I went. But when I looked inside there was only six apples, and that year there was a glut!

'The following week I went in the kitchen and saw Olive and told her, "I'm not goin' to skin any more hares for six apples. I thought I'd get at least a packet of cigarettes". But my comments were obviously noted because the followin' week I received a packet of fags through Olive.'

Later that year Fred bought his first new bike, 'a Sturmey Archer with three-speed and square mudguards, for £4 19s 6d'. The man who started out with a secondhand Raleigh was at last going places. But then history played a wicked hand.

In January 1939, when war looked imminent, Captain Gregg asked the keepers to join the Territorial Army, so Fred enlisted in their Royal Sussex Regiment. 'I did one night a week plus a minimum of one week's camp a year. I went to Eastbourne in the June, which was in the middle of the rearing season, so we thought it was wonderful. But to be fair to the shoot we didn't all go at the same time. Army life was not so good though.

'On the evening of Sunday 27 August I got my call-up papers and I had to report to Chichester Barracks next morning at 9am! I was put in the Royal Sussex Infantry for six years. I spent the first four in this country because I happened to be ill when we were due to go to France and they never took anyone who wasn't fit.

'Eventually I became a sergeant and went to Cairo and then on to five weeks' police duty at the Mena pyramids, where Churchill met Roosevelt. After that there was two years on convoy duty in the Persian Gulf, where the heat was terrible.

'When I was demobbed in 1946 I went to live with Freda at Horndean as we'd been married in 1942. The shoot had finished and the keepers paid off with a month's money at the start of the war, when farmers and Army blokes shot all the birds we'd carefully reared.'

Fred then did six months' casual labour for the Forestry Commission at Butser Hill, near Petersfield. 'Then an estate worker's job came up at Stedham Hall, Sussex, and as there was a house too I took it. But there was no way I could settle so I wrote off for various keepin' jobs. Unfortunately there was too many of us applying and you were lucky if you got anythin'. So I had to stay put for two years, during which time our daughter was born.

'Then in 1949 I was taken on by headkeeper Roberts on Cowdray Park, which adjoined Stedham and was just starting to feed birds on a small scale and build the shoot up again. I had a cottage and £3 a week plus sixpence a rabbit, but no suit. There were three of us keepers plus the head, who was also head forester, and that first season we reared about twenty coops between us. One odd thing was my Christmas box from the estate. It was 12/6d, consisting of 10s for me and half a crown for my wife!

'At the end of that season headkeeper Roberts retired after over fifty years and Lord Cowdray gave him a huge party in a marquee on the lawn at Cowdray House. All the estate workers were invited – foresters, grooms, keepers, the lot. There were about 300 of us and that was just the men! We had port wine to drink and you can guess the effect of that!

'But it was a terrible shoot at Cowdray. They shot on a Saturday and Monday, started at 9am and wouldn't stop till dark and you could see the flames comin' out the ends of the barrels. It was just too greedy, but Lord Cowdray said, "I don't shoot very often, but when I do I want a bloody good shoot". No matter what the weather was he never stopped. There were two lots of beaters but the bags were not that high, as it was soon after the war and there was no real stock yet. The Duke of Edinburgh came once when I was there and they picked out all the best drives for him.'

After two years at Cowdray, Fred's daughter was due to start school, but was faced with the prospect of a two-and-a-half-mile walk. 'So I asked the new head, Wiltshire, if we could move to a closer cottage. But he said no even though the

agent said yes. So I decided to leave at the end of the season.'

In 1952 Fred received a letter from headkeeper W. W. Wolfries, 'one of the hardest keepers I ever met, and I already knew him from Leigh Park. He wanted me to go to Stansted Park, Sussex, for £3 10s a week, which I did for four years, during which time our son was born. Earl Bessborough owned it, but he didn't shoot then so his son, Lord Duncannon, the present earl, ran it.

'I was one of two beatkeepers under Wolfries and this was the first place I'd ever had indoor sanitation, as well as Calor gas heatin' and light. Also, my daughter was picked up by school bus.'

Unfortunately, being close to several towns, Stansted was heavily poached. 'They mostly came out on foot from Emsworth and Leigh Park to get the pheasants with catapults on a Sunday in the daylight. There was not a minute's peace. It got so bad we had the police up there six weeks runnin' and ready for 'em, but they never came. They knew all right!

'The very first Sunday the police wasn't there the poachers came back. It was early in October and I saw this chap catapultin' pheasants along some wire netting. I crept up and jumped on his back. "OK, fair cop", he said, and admitted to me

(left) A helping hand: Fred assisted by his son John in 1957. (right) Master
and pupils: Fred (centre) has given several youngsters a good start in keepering

that he knew about the police presence. But at least I saw to it that he was fined
£10 plus costs.'

On the other hand, Stansted provided Fred with welcome variety of sport. 'We
killed a lot of woodcock there. Our best day was in January, when we killed thirty-
one, walking through a lot of bracken and birch scrub. Our main pheasant days
brought about 230.

'We also had great rabbit shoots there in February and March. On Tuesday and
Wednesday us two beatkeepers would go round and stink out the rabbits with
strips of paper dipped in Renardine and stuffed down the holes with sticks. On
the Thursday the headkeeper and local farmers would shoot up to 300, but we only
did the beating. Only once did Wolfries let me carry the .410, and that was only
because some rabbits were tucked up in a pit hole and wouldn't come out. I got
twenty and I don't think he liked it.

'Wolfries never expected you to have any time off for anythin'. Once I asked
if I could slip down to the village for a haircut and he said, "Ah! I need a haircut

too: we'll all go down in my car". But it was only to make sure we didn't slip off anywhere else.'

Each Christmas, Fred was delighted to receive £5 from Lord Duncannon, but found Wolfries far from generous. 'Us beatkeepers were never allowed up to the hall, where the tips were given. I always had to clean the guns at the head's house while Ron had to see to the dogs. When Wolfries came back he put only half the tips on the table and told us to share them out between the two of us. Even on the rabbit shoots, which he took part in, he took half the tips from a hat passed round by the farmers for Ron and me.'

In the end Wolfries' tough line was too much for Fred. 'He agreed that I could have an afternoon off to go to my brother-in-law's wedding, which was only local. So I worked till midday and arranged for Ron to look out for me later. The rest

Stinking out rabbits

of the family went off to the wedding by taxi while I cycled down with another brother-in-law. But we had to cycle past the headkeeper's lodge, and if he didn't see you she [his wife] did. So our movements was always known.

'So when it was time to come home, for a bit of devilment we cycled round the back way, even though it was another three miles. Then Wolfries couldn't see us come home. Next mornin' he was waitin' for me on the rearing field. "Keep the weddin' up all night then?", he said. "No, why?" I replied. Then he said, "I thought the least you'd have done was come back and help us shut the pheasants in". Well, I couldn't believe it, so we really fell out, and next night he gave Ron the evening off and made me shut up the pheasants on my own.'

Enough was enough. Fred told Wolfries that he would look for another job. So he wrote to the Game Research Station at Fordingbridge, and to Lowe's, Spratt's and James & Co, who all had registers of keepers, stating that he was interested in a single-handed vacancy.

'A week later I had a letter from Lord Monk-Bretton to say he had been sent my name and wanted to replace his keeper. I wrote back and then I had a second letter to say that he would be in the Hampshire area at Alton and could he call.

So he did, and saw my references and said, "Yes, I think you'll be suitable. And now I suppose you'd like to come to see the place." '

This looked a much better prospect altogether. Although Lord Monk-Bretton would not be at Conyboro, Cooksbridge, near Lewes, to show Fred round the estate on the appointed day, he arranged for syndicate partner Major Bradstock to be there. Furthermore, they even sent the car and chauffeur to fetch Fred and Freda from Lewes station. Everything went well and at last Fred found somewhere suitable to spend the rest of his working life – a further thirty-six years. 'This time I moved on 14 February!

'It turned out the previous keeper, who was the syndicate's first, had let them down badly with very poor returns over two seasons. Anyway, I bought 1,000 eggs from Lillywhite's and received the usual two and a half per cent extra for failures. In addition I got fifty eggs from the keeper on the adjoining estate, who I knew from Cowdray before the war. So I had about 1,100 eggs altogether.

'This was my first experience of rearing under the recently introduced Cotswold system. I thought it was marvellous because you didn't have to sit with the birds all day and shut 'em up at night. You had a run which was about 6ft long and 2ft wide and screwed onto the coop. The chicks could run about without fear of attack by winged vermin.

'All the eggs were hatched under broodies and as soon as the chicks had dried off they were transferred to the Cotswolds. They were fed and watered every day

Rural roots: Fred's birthplace at Elveden

for seven weeks. Then the coops were taken by tractor and trailer to covert and reassembled with the runs in the wood. The poults were kept in for twenty-four hours because they'd only seen half a human being before and had to acclimatise to a whole one, as well as the trees swinging about above. The following morning, after they were fed and watered, I just pulled the run away 6in from the coop so they could come out. Then I kept away till the evening feed. We bought six of those coops and runs and the estate carpenter copied them so we ended up with about fifty.'

All went well but Lord Monk-Bretton, understandably cautious after the previous year's fiasco, asked Fred if he would like a rehearsal for the first shoot. Equally understandably, Fred said, 'No, I think I know how a drive will go'.

When the big day arrived there were seven Guns and fourteen beaters, who received eighteen shillings and a pint of beer each. 'There was favourable weather and at the end of the day we'd killed 151 pheasants, compared with the last keeper's effort of 129 for the whole season – from the same number of eggs! Afterwards his lordship came up and congratulated me and gave me five shillings a week rise. We killed over 460 that season.'

After that successful start the shoot was gradually built up and took in more ground, totalling about 2,500 acres. Fred was given help by an old, retired groom and in later years various lads, who were obviously well trained because they went on to secure good positions. Among them was David Mason, who became headkeeper at Shadwell.

But the Conyboro years have not been without tales of the unexpected, not least

through the weather. 'In the first year we were moving birds to wood on the Thursday and on the Sunday there was a terrific gale. We were about fifteen miles from the sea but all around us the salt in the air turned the leaves brown just like autumn, as if someone had done it with a blowlamp.

'The following Monday week – August bank holiday 1956 – there was a tremendous thunderstorm with 6in of hail. Over at Barcombe cricket ground they 'ad a match which had to be abandoned because the hail was halfway up the stumps. At Arundel, roofs collapsed under the weight, some of the stones being as big as walnuts, and there was a 2ft-deep layer in the market square.

'In 1960 we were cut off for two days when there was a tremendous flood around Lewes. Vehicles floated away, people were trapped in upstairs rooms and they had to switch the power off at the station because the water was level with the platform. The passengers had to continue by bus.'

The torrential rain fell from 29 October to 4 November across southern England so inevitably it interfered with a lot of shooting. The Saturday was going to be Fred's big day of the season. 'We carried on but all the drives were messed up with Guns cut off and some falling in up to the neck.'

Three years later came England's biggest freeze-up in living memory. 'There was so much snow and frost none of the farm workers could work in early 1963 so they had to help me with the rabbitin'. But the drifts covered all the ditches and the dogs fell in. You could hear 'em goin' up and down but you couldn't see them, so we kept having to dig holes to get them out.'

Then came the hurricane of October 1987. Fred's house survived, but his greenhouse and sheds did not, which was a tragedy for a keen gardener (he still has an allotment). 'On the shoot, at the Golden Horn, where the king is said to have stopped for a rest and drunk out of a golden horn before attacking Lewes, only a dozen trees survived where before there were about 800. Elsewhere on the estate it was only really the softwood that suffered. But we found a lot of dead pigeons and doves and a few magpies. I think the foxes cleared up any dead pheasants before we found them, but we picked up a few injured birds.'

Fred Bayfield has certainly weathered many storms since those early Elveden days. He has also covered a great deal of ground and, apart from when he was in the Army, most of his adventures have been on foot or bicycle. His motor has been love of the outdoors and his fuel the simple desire to please. Still in good health and spirits, and living comfortably with Freda at Cuckfield in Sussex, he has no hesitation in saying he would do it all again, 'but it would have to be on four wheels next time'.

ROUGH AND READY

FRED LADHAMS

*ESSEX, LINCOLNSHIRE, NOTTINGHAMSHIRE,
OXFORDSHIRE AND CUMBRIA*

Being one of nine children in a struggling working-class family just after World War I, Frederick Ernest Ladhams had no easy upbringing. 'It was certainly rough and ready and the weak 'uns went to the wall.' But at least his tough childhood near London gave him the mental armour to cope with the rogues he would meet in later life.

The son of a foundry worker and grandson of a building labourer, Fred was born in a rented house on 31 January 1913, at Epping in Essex. 'There were no bathrooms then and father used to come home filthy, strip off to the waist and wash outside with water boiled over an open fire. I can still smell the carbolic soap.

'Now an insurance company's office stands on the site of our old house, but then it was all fields round about and I was always interested in the country.

'Our old headmaster at Epping Boys School used to let keeper Robin Taylor take about twelve to twenty of us beating at Copped Hall on a school day. There was no fixed age – all you had to be was big and strong enough. We got half a crown, a bottle of pop and two sandwiches – one saltbeef, the other cheese – which you could hardly get in your mouth.'

But although he allowed the boys to go off beating, the headmaster was, like most of his contemporaries, 'a real disciplinarian. You were caned for fighting and even if you was heard cheekin' someone in the town. Also, whenever the infants messed themselves, because they wasn't properly house-trained, us older ones had to take 'em out and clean 'em up. But the head and two masters lived at the school, where there was good gardens and we learned how to grow things and prune trees.'

Fred had several ways of earning pocket money. 'In those days there were lots of horses in London and I used to help uncle take hay and bedding down to them. When I was a bit older I was allowed to drive a second horse and cart down behind him. And on a Sunday I sometimes used to go down the local golf course to carry the clubs and get a bob or two.

'Also there used to be lots of wild flowers about Epping then. There was white and purple violets, peggles [cowslips], primroses and bluebells and we used to go and get 'em without the keeper seeing us. Then on a Sunday we used to sit out on the green and sell them to the cyclists for 3d a bunch. There were lots of cycling clubs came out of London then.'

In addition, Fred had the customary schoolboy's paper round for which he earned 1/6d a week. 'You 'ad to be thirteen and me and another lad 'ad to be down the station with a trolley to meet the half-six train. There were loads of other boys there and we all used to race downhill on our trolleys. My patch 'ad mostly the *Mirror*, the *Daily Herald* and the local rag, but in the higher up, posher districts there was papers like *The Times*.'

But there was also plenty of wildlife to interest a budding young countryman in Epping between the wars. 'Lots of fallow deer, of course, and always plenty of badgers and birds' nests to find. And all us boys and girls used to bathe together in a local pond. We took down a bar of soap and 'ad great fun. In them days you had to make your own entertainment.'

On leaving school at the age of fourteen, Fred replaced his older brother as boy keeper at Copped Hall, then owned by the 'very autocratic Mr Whyse and recently bought by pop star Rod Stewart. There was a massive staff then, including two chauffeurs for two Rolls Royces, three people in the laundry alone, and an old lady who made butter.

'The butter lady was given one cock pheasant each year. When I took it up to her she always put a shilling on the table in front of me, along with half a glass of port – good stuff that was. Each farm worker had an annual brace of rabbits but tenant farmers and local police had a brace of pheasants each.

'I was allowed to pick myself out two rabbits each week and at Christmas I always got a ticket from the squire for so much beef. The last one I 'ad was worth about 7/6d. Then I got a couple of dozen eggs a week and we used to collect

Teenager Fred Ladhams (right, with sack over shoulder) at Copped Hall, his first estate

blackberries for the squire at 6d a pound. Altogether I got about £4 for the berries and a woman used to come down from the squire's London home in Nightingale Square to collect them for jam etc. She also took back chickens, cream and other fresh produce.

'My wage was ten shillings to start and after seven years I was on twenty-five shillings. I always gave money to mum. I didn't get a suit of clothes till I'd been there three years.

'The headkeeper lived down in the Warren – a wood of big, old chestnut trees. I used to look after half his garden as well as the ferrets, chickens and dogs, including those Sealyham terriers for huntin' the wood out for rabbits. I even 'ad to clean the headkeeper's wife's brasses.

'Two or three days before a shoot I'd get a big bit of beef and cook it in a big, black pot in the copper house. This was for the beaters' sandwiches, each lot being wrapped in greaseproof paper. There was also coffee provided, and five-gallon casks of Whitbread's beer. The Guns always went to the shooting box and the butler and maid brought out their lunch from the hall.'

The estate pheasants were fed in the traditional way. 'Armitages of Nottingham was just startin' to fetch out that half-cooked feed then – all oily stuff. Most of it we cooked over an open fire and mixed in chopped rabbit. When the birds went to wood they was gradually weaned on to boiled corn cooked in the copper.'

*We used to collect blackberries
for the squire*

The shoot had just over 100 coops, each holding about fifteen birds, 'but I don't know the exact amount raised – the headkeeper never told you that! Anyway, the Guns killed about 200 a day then.'

Poaching was a considerable problem on London's doorstep. 'They was mostly after rabbits with snares, but we never stood any nonsense. Even if we walked on someone pickin' blackberries we tipped their basket upside down. You 'ad to be tough then and nip things in the bud. I even used to go down to some ivy trees, where birds was vulnerable, to drive pheasants out from roost so nobody could creep in and shoot them.'

Fortunately, natural predation was not a huge problem, 'though there were always plenty of foxes. There was just the odd crow and sparrowhawk, and that's where the grey squirrels first started to get about the country.'

In those days partridges were still common around Epping. 'One time in September, Mr Dashwood, the agent, and three Guns, with us four keepers and the gardener beatin', shot fifty brace of partridges. It was mostly English birds then and they were all wild. The cropping just suited 'em perfectly. You got your roots and you got your arable, with plenty of stubble left too. We generally walked the stubbles into a root field and the head blew a whistle to warn the Guns when birds got up.

'We 'ad some good Shots there. One of them was the local vicar, who later on married Iris and me. Her father worked in the foundry too.'

Another of Fred's sidelines at Copped Hall was, 'rearing about six litters of ferrets in the summer. We used to advertise them at ten bob each in *The Exchange and Mart* and I got a shilling for each one sold. We got enquiries from all over and often sent 'em to southern Ireland. The Irish stamps always came upside down on the envelopes. People used to say it was a deliberate insult to the Crown.'

At the age of twenty-one, in the spring of 1935, Fred left home for the first time, to become one of three underkeepers at Sir Fred Jones's Irnham Hall, near Bourne

Tea-break for
21-year-old Fred
on the Irnham
estate, Lincolnshire,
where the hours
were very long

in Lincolnshire. 'I only earned thirty-five shillings a week and paid £1 for lodging with the cowman, but meals was included. Iris joined me in 1936, when we were married; the gate lodge where we stayed was like a little castle.'

However, Fred was able to add significantly to his income through rabbiting, being paid 6d a couple for those caught. 'From September we started catchin' around the woods. We ran about 100 snares and it was much easier then because the stubble was left about 2ft high. It worked in well with your other jobs too because when we started the pheasants was just beginnin' to get off your hands. The butcher collected the rabbits and paid the estate and we were paid every four weeks. It often used to amount to a week's wages too.

'It was there I first learnt longnetting. We took out one 100yd net and two of 50yds, plus a bagful of hazel pegs. And your coat 'ad no buttons on so as not to snag the nets. You just had a thin cord round your waist. There was one man at each end of the net and you held the top line with your fingers so you knew when the rabbits hit. They were proper nets too – not like this modern rubbish which throws rabbits as soon as they get in.

'I always remember one night we set the three nets in a corner and later one of the smaller ones was missin'. Turned out there was so many rabbits hit it they carried the whole thing into the wood. There was only one setting a night, from about 10pm to midnight, and it was all carry then – very hard work. The rabbits was all gutted straightaway and we took a short spade to bury all the rubbish.'

There were some 150 coops of pheasants plus wild partridges at Irnham. 'They killed about 200–300 pheasants a day and in my first year they had a record fifty brace partridges on my beat. Sir Fred was eighty then and his chauffeur actually had to hold him under the arms while he shot. He died after I was there a year and then his son Walter took over.

'On a Saturday I used to pick up as many as 200 pheasant and partridge eggs along the roadsides. It was all arable there and they had tractors when everyone else was still using horses.

'Once the miners came out to plant a wood. The Government fetched 'em down in camps. When they came they was as thin and pale as that heater in the corner, but when they went back they was as tanned and healthy as anythin'.

'It was at Bulby Wood, which was supposed to be haunted, that I had the first instance of foxes being turned in on me [brought from another area and released] – for the hunt. There were three let go, but I shot 'em easily next morning as they were very tame. I'd seen their tracks in a sandbar along the beck. Later on they did the same to me in Oxfordshire, with a lot of big 'uns, but I nailed 'em all right. No way were we going to have foxes on the beat, hunt or no hunt!'

In 1937, at the age of twenty-three, Fred became underkeeper for Colonel Clifton at Clifton Hall, just south of Nottingham. 'We had to go to Beeston to be measured up for our suits – real Robin Hood jobs in Lincoln green.

'I got the job through the Gamekeepers' Association, but it was an awful place for poachers. They even used to creep round our bungalow at night to see if we were there talking.

'One night on roost watch this motorbike and sidecar went by us and later on, after we'd been home, we looked up and saw three fellows stickin' out like turkeys in the moonlight. We went up the wood to head them off, but there was not a twig crackin' or bird twitterin', so we went round the other end and then ran straight into 'em.

'The old one kept comin' in and comin' in. Then I left off to set after the others. When I caught them we 'ad a good set to and they threatened to shoot me, so I went back to help the head with the old boy. He still kept comin', but eventually the head 'it 'im with a stick and cut his face right open. Then we spun 'im round and got the cuffs on.

'Then we went back and got the car and chauffeur to take 'im down to Shire Hall at Nottingham. When we got him in the light there was blood all over the place and the sergeant said, "What the hell you been doin' with 'im?" He was a real poacher. His case came up just before Christmas and he got three months. We found out 'e was fifty-nine and he 'ad convictions goin' back to when he was a boy in 1890 – for everything from fowl stealing to pheasant poaching. His mates were in the court watchin' but we couldn't prove anything and they got away with it.'

Occasionally it was the keepers who came off worse. 'Once Johnny was cut right down the face by a longnetter's stick with a spike on the end. It really was a bad place and you 'ad to be watchin' all the time. As far as the birds was concerned, we always used to say that if you don't sleep with 'em you don't get 'em!

'Another time we were out in the moonlight when we heard thirty-six shots on nearby Thrumpton, the small place which Lord Byron used to own. Next day we went to see the keeper there and he said he'd been out and never got 'em. He claimed 'e challenged 'em and they dropped a bag with thirty-six pheasants in. But I said to Johnny Thomas, the headkeeper, "I reckon he stood off a bit because 'e was too scared".'

But at least the endless hours of nightwatching sometimes brought Fred light

relief. 'Once I was walkin' home in the bright moonlight and spotted this ol' bull-nosed Morris just turned off the road. There was a couple inside havin' a right old go – at 2am!'

While courting couples have entertained many a keeper, few have had such a surprise as that which lay in store for Fred when blanking-in Clifton Wood one day. 'We were goin' along nicely when one of the chaps called out, "'ey up Fred, there's a lass lays 'ere". So I went over and there she was, half under a bush. Her hair was perfect, but when we turned her over her face was half gone with maggots.

'The lads said, "What's to do Fred", so I said we'd carry on and beat the wood out as she wasn't goin' anywhere. Then after the drive I 'ad a conflab with the boss and he said we'd finish the shoot. When we got back we told the police but it was 10pm that night before the sergeant and a constable came knockin' on the door. Then we got the tractor and took 'em down. The sergeant poked about under 'er and found some bottles and a note. "Oh, it's a suicide", he said, "we don't bother

much about those." Anyway, we got her on a hurdle to carry her to the tractor. But what a stink! I made sure I was upwind when we took her up. A few weeks later I discovered that her fiancé had died suddenly – very sad.'

Fred had another encounter with tragedy at Clifton. 'We were goin' along the road lookin' for eggs when we came upon this old woman wringing her hands. She told us that her husband was missing and asked if we would help look around for him.

'Nearby was a stackyard with a well in the middle and I noticed a stick was on it. I said, "I bet he's in there", and sure enough 'e was – floatin' face down! He'd drowned himself and we found out later that they were going to put 'im in the infirmary, but he didn't want to go.'

Not surprisingly, Fred was keen to move on to pastures new, to gain valuable experience, and he was offered two positions when Clifton's headkeeper advertised on his behalf. So in the spring of 1939 he accepted a post at Blenheim, the Duke of Marlborough's estate in Oxfordshire. 'I took a partridge beat on the old Euston system and that really suited me.

'I had 200–300 dummy eggs and replaced the wild ones every second or third day. I put about twenty under a bantam and about thirty under a broody. Them as was in the most dangerous places was chipped off first. Before going to a nest I used to watch for the partridge to go off for her first feed at five or six o'clock in the morning, so as not to disturb her. This was very important. And at the same time I used to put Keating's flea powder in under the clutch, especially if you saw any blood spots on the eggs, which showed you the birds was lousy. You could always tell when the chicks were about to hatch because the cock would go and sit by the hen.

'Headkeeper Mr Grey was no worker, more of a gentleman who just rode around on a BSA 250 motorbike makin' sure everythin' was all right. And there was another chap who did nothing but fetch the feed for us keepers with his pony and trap.

'We might put out as many as twenty-one to twenty-two eggs in a nest – always as many as we could because the birds could always rear 'em better than you. Any Euston system eggs we couldn't get back out we used to rear ourselves, and we also bought about 100 Hungarian partridge eggs and put about two in each nest to change the blood. Our egg chipping bank was an old slate quarry.'

At that time Blenheim's agriculture was well suited to partridge production, providing plenty of natural food. 'We used to fetch the eggs for 'em from the ant 'eaps in the fields. When the sun was out the ants brought the eggs to the surface and then we took a spade to 'em and popped 'em in a bucket – just like slicing off a molehill. Baby partridges thrive on ant eggs, but you mustn't give 'em too many as they like 'em so much they might then refuse anything else. Blenheim was the only place I've been where we could do this. The 'eaps were on the rough grazing and Iris used to help me with them.

'Nowadays people just moan about the disappearance of the partridge, but if you want them back you've simply got to buckle down and look after 'em. Also you've got to strip every pheasant egg off a partridge beat as the pheasant is just like a cuckoo and will lay in every nest.

(left) The Cotswold rearing system was welcomed by Fred just after the war
(right) Fox control on the fells: Fred is assisted by his son

'Our house was pretty primitive at Blenheim, with all oil lamps and water from the well. The track down to it was a rough old thing and Iris used to say it shook all the nuts off the pram.

'I earned two guineas a week at Blenheim and was given the feed for thirty hens, which kept us in eggs. My leggings was brown leather, whereas they were boxcloth

back in Lincolnshire. And I had a black bowler which I was supposed to wear all the time, but whenever I could I only wore it on shoot days because you looked a real case in it.

'They was very strict then and you only spoke to the duke when you was spoken to. Your hat 'ad to come off pretty smart and you didn't 'ave to 'ave a fag on your lip. Nowadays they get away with murder. But at the same time a keeper was really somethin' in the community then.'

Notwithstanding the strictness of the regime, Fred soon settled in and produced the required results. 'When they shot my beat in September 1939 they got 100 brace and ninety per cent were young. Actually the Guns killed ninety-five brace, so the headkeeper told me to take some cartridges and go out in the morning to get another ten birds so that it would look better in the gamebook. Nobody knew any different.'

There was some superb shooting at Blenheim during Fred's time. 'With two lines of beaters there was never any hanging about. There were only four big-bang drives – two in the morning and two in the afternoon. Combe Bottom was fantastic – no bang-bang and then a space like at most places. The birds came out like clouds of starlings and in 1939 they shot 400 on just that one drive when there was 1,500 pheasants for the day. I think it must have been some sort of record at the time because I remember there was a fair bit of jealousy with Lord Derby's Knowsley Hall. But there were some crack Shots to get the bags. The then duchess was one of the best I've seen. It was all double guns.'

The duke too was a keen Shot. 'Even if anyone missed on his family day, when they went round in an old bus, he used to shout at 'em, "If you can't hit them you might as well go home". He was a great big feller who used to march straight through the irrigation channels followed by his very short loader carrying his gun over his head. It was very comical. And there was a model railway at the palace which was supposed to be for the young marquis, but the duke spent most of his time on it.'

One of the Guns stands out in Fred's memory for his political associations rather than sporting prowess. 'It was Duff Cooper, the ambassador to France. I stood behind him all morning, but at lunchtime he 'ad to go back to France with all the carry on.

'Later on they tried to get us Blenheim keepers to form a special brigade of territorials, but in the end, with the war, all rearing stopped and in spring 1940 everyone of service age had to leave. So then Iris and me went back to Essex and I had just odd jobs – mostly building tank traps – before I was called up.'

In due course, Fred was summoned to Walthamstow for a medical and was 'pronounced A1, but they always gave you the opposite of what you wanted to do. Three weeks later I was called up to Exeter and then posted to Blandford, Dorset, as part of the Royal Artillery Searchlight Regiment – 546 Battery. There were about eleven men on a small site and thirty-three on a big one. The big one picked up the planes and the small one zoomed in on it.'

In 1941 Fred was posted to Northern Ireland, 'to Dunoon in the Antrim Hills around Belfast, where there were miles of heather and I saw my first grouse as well as lots of brown trout in the tarns. We stayed there till the summer of '43, but

there was not much doin'. I never saw a single keeper when I was goin' around the woods and most of the lads with me there came out of London and had never even seen a tree let alone a pheasant. But one good thing over there was that they would give you anything as long as you 'ad the money to pay for it. There was never any worry about coupons.

'After that we went to Hull, Bath, Bristol and York, before the regiment broke up and we joined the 68th Searchlight Regiment, billeted on Bath racecourse. Then we were sent to Lord Mostyn's place at St Asaph in North Wales, where we went down the woods and at last met a keeper. He spoke real broad Welsh and we got on well.

'After that we were in Palestine, Syria, Turkey, Lebanon and Egypt, where I saw the Frankie Howerd show in Cairo. In those days you could go to the Forces Club there and they'd make up a £1 parcel to send home for you, though it took six weeks. It was mostly sweets such as sugared almonds and Turkish delight, but someone popped a banana in mine. When it arrived the banana was still green so Iris hung it up in her mum's sittin' room, but it never did ripen. Our son had never seen a banana before.'

Although he was only thirty-one, Fred then decided that he was too old for the infantry and, 'wangled it to go in the cookhouse', eventually leaving the Army as a private in 1946, without any regrets. 'I tell you what – England's the place to be. When we were on the boat comin' home there was an announcement saying,

"Anyone want to see the white cliffs of Dover?" Well, it's a wonder the boat didn't turn turtle there was such a rush to one side.'

The war years had been far from pleasant for Iris too. To begin with, when the Ladhams moved from Blenheim to London the pipes in their house froze, eventually bursting and causing such damp their first son died of pneumonia at only two years old. And when Fred was abroad Iris had a telegram to say he was missing. 'But it turned out he had a touch of malaria and was in hospital, where they mixed him up with another chap. And they never paid me any pension while he was missing!'

When Fred left the Army he had accrued ten weeks' paid leave. 'I was free as a bird and I took every day of it. But I always intended to go back to keepering. I wrote to Blenheim and Nottingham, but it was dead there so I asked keeper Johnny Thomas to advertise for me. I ended up going to Lowther, near Penrith, in July 1946, under headkeeper William Semple, and remained there till I retired.

'Viscount Lowther was a bit autocratic   just like it was before the war. He used to ride around on a big, white horse and every Sunday for a few weeks before the season opened he'd get the keepers out and walk in line with us just to see what the grouse was like. He was a very keen Shot and hated shooting any gamebird up the arse. He died of cancer at fifty-nine.

'There were some real characters about then. One old farmer – Isaac Cookson from Sceough Fell – used to cut the bracken for cattle bedding using a long-handled corn scythe and bring it down with a sledge drawn by a Galloway pony. He also took the ling for his fire. His long, white beard was tucked into his belt, and when he took his home-made butter to Penrith market people was scared to sit beside him on the bus.'

Fred's first beat at Lowther was Buck Holme Woods, but later he had others. 'And the 6,000 to 7,000-acre Helton beat, between Ullswater and Haweswater, had it all, with red deer, roe deer, blackgame and partridges as well as grouse and pheasants.

'The whole estate was about 70,000 acres and some 50,000 was shot. One season we 'ad forty shoot days on grouse and pheasants and none was reared. Also only cock pheasants was shot because the Viscount said it was best to leave the hens. When I had Buck Holme we shot 119 cocks. Well, it was 120 with one hen – a very dark bird, bagged by Chief Constable Brown of Cumbria, but he did apologise for his mistake.'

When Fred arrived at Lowther he joined an ageing team. 'I was one of the first new blood. We were paid on the first Monday of the month and when I went up for it I was like a baby compared to all the others. Before that I'd been paid fortnightly. My wages was £3 5s plus 2s a day shoot lunch money, 1s a week each for keeping two ferrets, 3/6d a week each for two retrievers and 1/6d a week for a terrier. The dog and lunch money was paid every six months and they made you sign in a book for it. The secretary was old John Peel – a descendant of the real one.

'Viscount Lowther ran the estate for the sixth Earl – Lance, and when he died the grandson James took over very young as the seventh Earl. So then I worked for the Hon Captain Lowther. It stayed entirely a private shoot till 1949 and we used to shoot for six days solid from the 12th. The third year I was there we killed 168 brace on Shap.

'I used to load for Viscount Lowther and 'e was a strict ol' boy in the butt. One day 'e asked me whether it was thirteen or fourteen grouse he 'ad down and I said I wasn't quite sure. He said, "You should bloody well know – that's why you're here". But next time round he asked for me again, so I couldn't have done that badly.

'It was nothin' to get fourteen to twenty birds round a butt in them days, but you 'ad the Guns then! The best grouse Shot I saw was Sir John Jardine, who used to fetch 'is headkeeper with 'im for a week. But they all used to have their own valet/loaders with 'em.'

During Fred's time at Lowther the estate held coursing meetings. 'We used to go round to the other estates and net hares to bring in. There was never too much trouble with poachers as once a year Captain Lowther used to give the gypsies – about forty to fifty of 'em – a Sunday runnin' greyhounds at hares on Askham Fell. Shocker Bowman used to get 'em all together and they would bet against each other. That kept 'em happy for a twelve month. The seventh Earl stopped all that.

'But there used to be quite a bit of trouble with salmon poachers on the river. So one day in my second year we were joined by three water board fellers and I got another young chap to help. We saw a light comin' down to the swing bridge

Fred and Iris Ladhams with their son Trevor on Askham Fell in 1946

and there were some men either side of the river. We were in a hollow and you could 'ave 'eard 'em comin' at Penrith they made so much noise.

'Then suddenly they were there, looking huge on the skyline above. One chap 'ad a gaff and two salmon over his shoulder, so I went for 'im and grabbed him round the waist. But my mate Brodie jumped on top of me and the others didn't come in, so we only got the one. It cost 'im sixteen guineas, but 'e said, "Will you take a cheque?" The fine was nothin' to 'im. He made hundreds out of salmon durin' the war, and they were great big fish then. Still, it was hell of a shock to 'em as they'd been gettin' away with it for years, and things quietened down a bit after that.'

Sometimes Fred also had to take people stalking. 'One chap was so excited at shooting a royal 'e left 'is glasses on the spot. But when he told me it was too dark to do anythin' about it. So next morning I took a couple of others up there to search for 'em. Well, we were just walking up the moor in line when I saw the glasses glinting in the sunlight. He were a lucky chap.

'We also used to take the occasional two-year-old pricket stag in and fatten it up for the castle – just like raisin' a steer.'

Like so many keepers, Fred first had a motorbike for transport. 'It was a BSA 125 which ran on Petroil and you could take it anywhere.' Then he had a Bond three-wheeler car, 'which you 'ad to kick-start on a cold morning because the battery was hopeless.'

Later on, Captain Lowther's Whitbysteads syndicate bought Fred a new, M-registration Robin Reliant, the 3-wheeler being popular because it could be driven with only a motor cycle licence. 'I had that for four years and then they bought me another new one for £900, and fourteen years ago a third for £3,000. I still had the Robin when I retired and did not give it up until 1990. I even used to take it out on the grouse moor, but the only trouble was in snow, when you couldn't follow the tracks of the other vehicles.'

The worst winter that Fred could remember was that of 1946–7. 'It was the July before all the snow went at Haweswater and our house was completely cut off for three weeks. You could only just see the tops of some of the telegraph poles and our only fuel was some dead oak trees which we cut down. We were down to our last cup of flour before they dug us out. Then just after I managed to get out for some supplies the wind got up and blew the snow back in again. It was no good shootin' a rabbit as they was all skin and bone. And thousands of sheep were wiped out on the fells, but it was a good year for carrion crows with all the dead meat to feed off.'

But despite all the hardships, Fred Ladhams, 'would do it all again. After all, there were plenty of good times. And I've been all over with the bosses loadin' – it was just like bein' on holiday with your keep found.'

Fred retired in 1978, but did a further two years part-time for the Lowther estate. He and Iris are still close to the Cumbrian countryside, in a block of retirement flats in the small market town of Kirkby Stephen, not too far from their two sons – a head gardener and a police sergeant – and grandchildren. But the days of stripping off to wash outside are long past.

A Proper Yorkshireman

Newton Hutchinson

YORKSHIRE AND DURHAM

Even along the Pennines, where chill winds have bred a tough race, few people are more outspoken than 80-year-old Newton Hutchinson. Proudly he describes himself as, 'a proper Yorkshireman'. Yet no one could take offence at his colourful language because the ever-present twinkle in his eye reveals the great kindness and friendliness for which Dalesmen are also renowned.

Named after a relative, Newton was born on 28 June 1913, at Arkengarthdale, Reeth, near Richmond. At first he lived with his grandfather, who was a miner, but was greatly influenced by his gamekeeper uncle. And he was always close to the land because, 'in those days all miners and most keepers 'ad a bit of ground, with a cow. That was the wife's living. And every garden 'ad vegetables in. Now when I go back it surprises me to see all the roses.

'We never 'ad a lot, but we managed to eat quite well. The butcher came out once a week with 'is pony and trap. Then the farmers used to keep these wee, "shot", unsaleable lambs and when one was killed it was divided up between everyone. Also, grandad always kept a pig or two – everyone did.

'Everybody in the dale could put their hand to somethin' and me ol' grandad was specially good at killin' a pig. This was generally on a Monday because it was washday for a farmer's wife and she already 'ad the copper on for the scaldin' and cleanin' up after. Pig-killin' day was a real friendly do. They always 'ad these five-gallon kegs of beer so they was 'appy as pigs in China.

'Grandad cured the pigs, and made all the sausages an' all. In those days a farmer's wife would send a lad up to you with a big hanky tied round a plate with bits of all the meats off the pig on it. That was her sign of friendship. There was only one feller used to grumble, and 'e was the butcher!

'There were about eighty-four of us children at school, from all over Arkengarthdale. It was big families in them days.' However, Newton was one of only three children. 'My brother Nigel became a keeper on Reeth moors and my sister went to Newcastle to work in munitions.

'The school bus was one of only two motor vehicles in the dale and it took children who lived over three miles away, but I was bloody unlucky because I was two and three-quarter miles off and told to walk. But one of the two drivers was a grand feller and would always pick us up anyway. Now the dales have changed tremendous with all the transport.

'Our two school-teachers were very

strict, but I was always a little devil. I never used to go when I was sent for the stick, which was a lot. I just used to go out in the porch, rub my hands and come back pretendin' to cry. But I was found out in the end when the teachers compared notes.'

Unfortunately, the lure of the wild was too much for Newton to bear. 'If I knew they were off foxing I'd put my hand up and say, "Please sir, can I leave the room?" Then as soon as I was out of sight off I'd go. But at least I always beat the others when it came to questions on nature – leaves, nests and everythin' else. We used to be taken on nature walks.'

Before Newton's time there was a lead mine in the dale. 'But then we 'ad this mine for chert [a flintlike form of quartz]. Old man Ward used to carry it away in great big blocks. His motor wagon – the second vehicle in the dale – had solid tyres and he used to give us all a lift to Richmond Station to go on our Sunday school trips. Richmond was part of the LNER then, and end of the line.'

During his school-days Newton used to help his uncle with cleaning the kennels, heather burning and other keepering jobs, mostly on a Saturday morning. 'Uncle was very strict with everyone. On a shoot day he used to say to the pony boys, "Eh! You don't need two to watch these ponies, one of you get on down there flanking". Then as soon as the firing was over you 'ad to be back down there at the right place for your gent.'

Newton left school at the customary age of fourteen. 'There was no advertisin' in them days – you were kind of 'anded down with jobs. Anyway, I 'ad the chance of two keeper positions – one at Bowes under Len Forester, and another at Malham Tarn, way over Masham country. But they meant I 'ad to leave home and you didn't like leavin' the dale, it was such a friendly place. Mind you, every man that's left has done very good, becoming policemen, keepers, etc, because I think the gentlemen knew we were all honest and trustworthy. And bein' a Hutchinson I was never refused a job.

'So I stayed at 'ome and did a bit of haytiming, rabbit catchin' etc – anythin' to get a bob or two. The farmers paid me about £1 a week for the rabbits, which I caught with snares and ferrets – boltin' and shootin' 'em. The rabbits was sold at Richmond. It was the farmer's wife's livin' then, 3d a couple for shot rabbits and 6d a couple for snared.

'But I did all sorts, includin' burnin' timber for one chap at Marske. And I was always out on shoots – the keepers really took to me. They knew I could take round a dozen beaters and know just where to put them. I suppose it was a sort of gift. But you could never get grouse beaters then unless all the farmers had already got their haytime in.

'We were always gettin' together to shoot the foxes in the dale. The horses couldn't hunt there. It were that rocky they'd 'ave killed theirselves. I 'elped the keepers with this and we all got on together. Now where there's one keeper there used to be six.'

Newton was 'about twenty-three' before he took his first full-time keepering job. 'We were havin' bait [lunch] by a wall. There would 'ave been the usual mincemeat and taties in pastry, a cold bottle of tea (no flasks then man!), and perhaps a bit of cake or gooseberry pie. Then the headkeeper of Marske says to me, "When you

gettin' married, Newton? I want an underkeeper." So I said, "I'll 'ave a go at both".

'So off I went to Marske, halfway between Reeth and Richmond, where my wages was three shillings short of £2. I 'ad a suit and a free house, but if you wanted wood you 'ad to get it yourself. The suit was "nigger" brown. The headkeeper gave us the cloth in a roll and you could 'ave any tailor you wanted. We was allowed £5 to make it up and I had Mr Clay from Leeds. He used to travel all round the farms and was a very good tailor. We 'ad a cap too, but I was always bein' pulled up for not wearin' mine. I had lovely curly hair in them days.'

At Marske, Newton's headkeeper was Milton Beattie from Northumberland, 'a grand feller. There were two of us underkeepers and a pheasant lad. The boss was Mr Martineau, who rented the shoot from D'arcy Hutton.

'We worked on both grouse and pheasants, and the rearin' was all broodies then.

We used to buy the hen cluckers for 18d each if they sat, and if they didn't we very soon took 'em back. When they was finished we sold 'em for 3/6d to anyone as they'd lay their heads off.

'The boss used to come for six weeks. He was an American millionaire. But it was her [Mrs Martineau] that 'ad the money. She was a little devil.

'One day the head said to me, "When you go up to check your butts over take your gun and shoot a grouse". So I did, and put it in me pocket on shoot day as instructed. Meanwhile, the head met the boss by the hall to see how the wind was, to choose the beats. He always went by the weathercock.

'Away we went on my patch and eventually Mrs Martineau says to me, "There's a grouse down over there Hutchinson". But the boss said there wasn't. Anyway, I had to go with her to look for it. Then the headkeeper signalled me with his whistle and when she wasn't looking I dropped the grouse I 'ad in my pocket. After a bit she said, "Look Hutchinson, here it is". So I sent Silk for it and he retrieved to me before she could touch it.

'We took the grouse back to the boss, but he knew what was goin' on. He felt the bird and whispered to me, "Look Hutchinson, it's cold. Never mind, you've put her in good tune" – yummer that is. And after that I couldn't do a thing wrong. You had to be cute then – tricks of the trade, boy.'

But it was certainly a hard life at Marske. 'From the 12th of August you 'ad to be up at 5am and over there, on parade – all black boots and done up – for the off at 9am. I often had to walk two miles four times a day on the pheasants and it was six miles to get to your moor. It was all shoemucker's gallowa' [shanks's pony] then. And every fourth day I 'ad to sit up all night watching, no matter if I were tired from the day before. Nowadays these keepers don't know they're born. It's the Land-Rovers that's spoiled it. In the old days you was out all day with your bottle of tea and you'd often walk miles before you even saw the heather.

'One day the head came and said, "You've got to go and see the little bugger". So I reported to Mrs Martineau and found out she wanted to take me to London to train dogs for her. But I didn't want to go, so I said to her, "Is there any heather there?" "No", she said. So I said, "Well, it's no good then", and I stayed at home.

'We had all black labradors then and all the good dogs were mine. It was nothin' for someone to pay £100 for a good animal then. They were good guard dogs too. When the pheasant lad was sent to fetch the baits [lunches] he could never get mine. My dog wouldn't let 'im anywhere near it!

'After a while the boss said we all 'ad to wear plus-fours, but I said to the others, "To hell with that, we've always 'ad breeches". Anyway, in the end we 'ad to 'ave them, and when I put them on, my wife, who used to knit my stockings, said I looked a fool. But my neighbour said to me, "Newton, you do look grand". Well, I was turning round in 'em and I thought someone was followin' me, they was so wide. Then I went over to the hall in 'em and one of the valets came over to me and said, "Good morning Mr Beattie". Then he realised who it was and said, "Good God, it's Hutchinson: you do look grand". That was in 1938, and from then on I wore plus-fours to the day I retired from full-time keeperin' in 1979.'

It was at Marske that Newton encountered the finest Shot he has ever seen. 'We 'ad lots of grouse there but nobody could 'it 'em much, so one day Beattie said to Martineau, "I wish you'd get some better Shots in". Anyway, this 12th of August the wind was just right for my beat. After a bit Beattie says to me, "There's a man down there gone wild. I know I used to moan nobody could 'it anythin', but after 'im there won't be a grouse left on the place". Turned out it was Guy Moreton.

'Next day we 'ad to go over to Reeth moor to help and the same team of Guns was there. The poor ol' head up there – Jack Alderson – was cryin' they shot so many. My God, Guy Moreton didn't 'alf belt some grouse down. It was all double guns then. They 'ad colossal bags. But Colonel Guy Wilson – the owner of Arkengarthdale estate – was a brilliant Shot too.'

In 1939 Newton was visited by 'an old brigadier who used to shoot with us. He said, "You'll be for the call up soon. You want to go and join the Royal Ordnance." So off I went to Leadenhall Street, Darlington. It was the first time I'd been to the town.

'At Darlington I wanted a smoke so badly I went into this shop with a Capstan sign and asked this lass if she could spare a packet of fags. Then two little kiddies came out and said, "Eh, it's the gamekeeper from Marske". They remembered me from when I let them go down to the waterfall. So after that their mum let me 'ave twenty Capstan, not just ten.

'When I arrived at Leadenhall Street there was keeper John Lambert from Coverdale there too. He'd been on the beer and when he 'ad to pee in the glass 'e filled it up so full it splashed all over when the doctor picked it up. Then 'e was passed grade two because 'e 'ad great big flat feet.

'After that a lad said to Lambert, "By gum, you've got a hairy chest", so Lambert thumped 'im right in the chest and 'e went flyin'. Then, when I was bein' sworn in, this specialist came rushin' out and said, "Stop, there's been a mistake". I was passed unmedically fit [unfit] for all forces because I'd had rheumatic fever as a lad. When I 'ad it I was wrapped up with cotton wool all around me to sweat it out. Mother looked after me and there was no penicillin in them days.'

Newton gratefully returned home to Marske, later discovering that the crafty brigadier had only recommended the Royal Ordnance because he was already in it and wanted the keeper he knew well to be his batman!

'In those days Beattie used to go to Grinton pub, near Reeth. When he was drunk he rode 'is motorbike fine, but as soon as 'e got off 'e fell flat on 'is back. At night you could see 'is light snakin' up those big 'ills. Anyway, one night I was ridin' pillion and when we got to the top of the hill I heard *boom boom*. So I said, "There's sumat goin' on, we'd better stop, what with the light an' all". "Bugger it", he said, "we'll press on." So we did, and on the Monday we 'eard that some bombs 'ad been dropped right on our moor – Copperthwaite, near Marrick.

'Poor old Beattie couldn't smell foxes or hear properly, you know. He was a gunner in the first war and suffered a terrible shock which left 'im like it.

'Another time at Marske, one sunny day in June, I 'eard this *pip pip pip* on Skelton moor and looked up to see a Spitfire after a German plane, which came down on Barnard Castle.

'Then there was a day when the air raid warden was blowin' 'is whistle all over the place and there was a big fire on the moor. I met Walter Lee – the Barningham keeper – and we ran up the valley together to see what was goin' on. Suddenly this great big airplane engine came rushin' down through a stone wall right by us. Further up we found two Germans on the ground still in their seats, all bloody and their legs smashed up. The rest of the plane was all over the place – there'd be bits there yet. And I bet the wall's still down where the engine just missed us.

There were one or two sheep killed too.'

During the war Newton volunteered as a special constable at Richmond. 'It was a good job. They sent me round all the gentlemen's houses to make sure all their lights were out. Some of 'em were shootin' men I already knew and they used to look after me. One feller used to leave a bottle of beer out for me every night.

'Bein' a special helped me enormous with the poachin'. The local inspector used to put all the newly-wed police on duty at Marske and tell 'em, "You've got some good friends there – that's the keepers". And if they put a foot wrong he'd send 'em off to Catterick Camp or some other place where there was some real thievin'.'

Eventually, 'Marske was sold and the farmers bought their farms when the Martineau lease was up. Sir James Baird of Middleton Lodge took the shooting. Only the headkeeper was kept on and it was arranged for me to replace Beattie when he retired. But they didn't sack me. D'arcy Hutton was very good to me and said that I was not to be thrown out of my house.'

Newton's letter of appointment at Raby

> TELEGRAPH AND TELEPHONE—STAINDROP 207.
> STATION WINSTON, N.E.R.
>
> RABY ESTATES OFFICE,
> STAINDROP,
> DARLINGTON,
> Co. Durham.
>
> KAC/JA   23rd July, 1954.
>
>
> Dear Sir,
>
>   I am glad to be able to confirm
> that Lord Barnard has agreed to your appointment as keeper
> on the Selaby Hall Beat of the Raby Estate.
>
>   I confirm therefore that you are
> appointed Keeper at a wage of £6.10.0d per week, less
> National Health Insurance and in addition, you will get
> TWO loads of logs per annum, plus the usual rates for
> dog keep prevailing on the Estate.
>
>   With regard to the house, I shall
> have to let you know as soon as possible when it is vacant
> but hope we will be able to have it in a month and in the
> meantime, I should be glad if you confirm if you are
> prepared to accept the position and let me know when you will
> be free.
>
>   Yours faithfully,

However, without any regular income, Newton was forced to look for a job. 'I opened the *Stockton and Darlington Times* on the Saturday and saw, "Wanted – gamekeeper – Barnard Castle district. Apply A. W. Watts, Northallerton." He was Major Morrit's agent for Rokeby.

'On the Sunday I told Beattie about it and on the Monday 'e took me on 'is motorbike to see our agent, Benjamin Taylor of Leyburn. Taylor just picked up the phone and arranged for me to meet A. W. Watts at the Morrit Arms.

'I went to the interview by bus, all expenses paid. When I arrived there was half a dozen of us picked out, all walkin' up and down in front of the pub, not much said. Then I was recognised and one of the others said, "Oh no, it's a Hutchinson; he'll get the job – we might as well go home".

'When I saw the agent 'e said, "By God, you're a big feller". I said, "I'm not to cross". Then we soon got down to brass tacks – house, money etc. So I started there in 1940, for about the same wages as before, just the headkeeper and me, apart from when his son joined us later. Major Morrit was a grand Shot, and a tiptop fly man. He wrote several books about fishin' and 'e was a good painter.'

But things did not always go smoothly at Rokeby. 'Once the major 'ad some guests over on leave and 'e decided 'e would let them shoot on the Sunday as the game laws was changed specially for the war. Well, it was the only time in my life I've shot on a Sunday and I didn't like it one bit. Sunday was Sunday. To ask a man to turn out after he'd done six days a week – well! Still, it didn't 'appen again.'

Bags at Rokeby were about 100 – all pheasants. 'We managed to do a bit of feedin' durin' the war as we gave the farmers a day's rabbitin' and they gave us the rakin's off the fields.'

Although Newton was at Rokeby for eight years, he did not really like it there. 'People used to say, "How's that keeper got out the war?" I always said we should 'ave 'ad badges sayin' medically unfit for service.

'We 'ad a lot of poachers from Barnard Castle too. They always said they was pickin' mushrooms but they was really settin' snares for rabbits. Mind you, we 'ad a few at Marske as well. But it's all part of the game. There was a clique at Richmond did it for the money and you 'ad one or two scraps. But in those days we were police on the land, you know. The real police couldn't even come on the estate without your say so.

'I've never been injured by poachers. I've always waded in first. If I struck at someone runnin' away it was always at their ankles. Then they dropped like a rabbit.'

Not surprisingly, some of Newton's assailants ended up needing medical attention. 'But my old doctor – Williams at Richmond – never 'ad much sympathy for 'em as they was in the wrong. He was a shootin' man and never sent me a bill – even when my boy 'ad pneumonia. He always said 'e'd take it out of someone who 'ad money.'

In 1948 Newton was told, 'to go for a single-handed keeper's job at Clervaux Castle, Croft, near Darlington. I was there for four years, for C. W. D. Chater, solicitor. It was poached to death. I caught about six or eight a week and got it squared up like, but you were never done. It was all pheasants, partridges and duck, and I didn't like it there.

'Then one day this police sergeant – I. Hanson from Middleton St George, near Darlington – came to the lodge. He said, "I've been lookin' for you for years". He'd been keeper boy long before me back at Rokeby and 'e 'eard they wanted a keeper at Raby. The police sergeant there 'ad been askin' around and Hanson said I was highly recommended.

'They wanted me in the cabin at Raby, but I didn't like it and turned it down. So they asked me to go to Selaby. That was poached and trespassed to death, but I took it and it was the best place I ever 'ad. I went there in 1954 and for the first time ever I 'ad a bathroom and runnin' water out of a tap. There was even fire logs – everythin' I wanted. It suited me fine and I stayed there till I retired, twenty-six years later. Back in the dale the water ran off the hill into a stone trough 100yds from the house and you 'ad to take a bucket and cup to it.'

Putting up with relatively primitive domestic conditions was all the more remarkable when you consider the hard winters which high-ground keepers and their families have often had to endure. The worst that Newton can recall was that of 1946–7, when he was at Rokeby. 'Cut off? Good God man! My wife and children nearly starved. When it was over I think we just finished with only a chair and table in the house. We 'ad to use everythin' we 'ad to keep warm. It took me half a day rather than half an hour to get down to Barnard Castle. When I got there I bought a three-gill bottle of paraffin and a bit of flour and yeast – that was about all I could carry. There was a hell of a lot of dead sheep on the moor

The Robin Reliant three-wheeler played a great part in Newton's keepering life

'There was a bad time in early '63 too. After a good breedin' season there was a lot of wild English partridges at Selaby, so we brought some of 'em into the hall and Lady Barnard was tryin' to warm 'em up and dry 'em out by the fire.'

When he started at Raby, Newton, 'reported to the Right Honourable John Vane, Lord Barnard's son, who had the shoot at Selaby. He's now Lord Barnard. The first Lord Barnard never shot. He was a big huntin' man.'

'People often say to me, "How did you get the job at Raby?" and I always say, "Good manners". In the old days if I was comin' up the lane and saw someone pass me who was older than me I had to raise my cap. That's how it was then. You always showed respect.' Indeed, I am reliably informed by Newton's son Brian, that hat protocol was so ingrained in his father's character he even put his cap on to answer the telephone for the first six months after it was installed!

But for all his good manners, Newton insists that he, 'never got a tip till I came to Raby, where I became second keeper'. Even then he was generally more impressed by people's integrity and skill than their money. One of the great highlights of his life was when he shook hands with Prince Charles, who came to hunt locally. 'Lord Barnard said to me a while later, "I hear you've met Prince Charles". I said, "Yes milord, and I've not washed my hand since, though it were a month ago".'

However, not all celebrities have created the right impression. 'When I was loading at Lowther I met Charlie Drake, the comedian, who was shootin'. He 'ad two silly pheasant tail feathers in his hat and was squeakin' all over the place. In the end he was shoutin' so much and spoilin' the drives the head told him to shut up.'

Many Guns, not least those in his employers' families, have benefited from Newton's coaching over the years. He knew what he was talking about, too, having been a first-class Shot himself. He often won clayshooting competitions, 'including the Holwick [now at High Forest] several times. I've always said that a gent's gun

should be choked first barrel and cylinder second. And he should shoot the birds where they gang, not where they been.

'Tell you the truth mister, I never really liked shootin' game because I was brought up to believe that the game's the boss's and the vermin's the keeper's. I used to get 3/6d for a stoat, 1/6d a weasel and 5s for a fox, from Horace Friend, the dealer. We 'ad to do that to buy a few cigarettes.'

In pest control Newton was always a great believer in traps. 'They was catchin' 'em while you were sleepin'.' His favourite was the 'Samson', a simple, home-made, dead-fall device in which the victim dislodges a baited wooden-peg support and is trapped under a stone slab. 'See all these slabs in the yard. There's one there for every size up to cat, and they've all caught well.'

Despite his praise of the past, Newton has not been against all modern inventions. After years of walking everywhere he was certainly glad to get some motorised transport of his own. 'I 'ad a motorbike first, a Norman 2-stroke which cost £21. People could 'ear me comin' for miles around and I passed me test on it. After that I 'ad a brand-new BSA 250. Then I bought a BSA 600. By hell, that could move and I caught many a poacher on that. But as I got older I got a bit cold on the bike so I bought a Robin Reliant three-wheeler, which I 'ad for twenty-one years.'

Neither was Newton devoted to *all* the old methods of keepering. 'I didn't particularly like the Euston system for partridges. It's OK on a small patch, but not where you've got five or six thousand acres. You can't keep proper control of the nests then. No, I was a vermin man first.

'At Marske all the keepers that came along for a job could shoot OK, but when the head sent 'em to me to check, they hadn't got a clue when settin' a trap. You've got to camouflage to make it natural. And I used to spend a lot of time studyin' the vermin, mister. You watch for all the signs. Listen to that blackbird – *plop plop plop* – he's tellin' you somethin's there.'

One of Newton's keepering mementos, ideally suited to his impish sense of humour

Newton welcomes the local hunt at his home on The Green, Piercebridge

Today Newton still takes a close interest in the wildlife around his home on The Green, at Piercebridge. He retired to the yellow-washed cottage, which bears the Barnard estate crest, in 1979. But with blood circulation problems now he rarely travels far, preferring to sit outside, enjoying the magnificent garden now tended by son Brian, or reflecting on old times at the splendid George Inn, where Dick Turpin is said to have hidden. Indeed, he has become almost a landmark within the village, one who always keeps an eye on things. 'If anybody goes away here they always come and tell me.'

Newton did not plunge into full retirement. Indeed, the estate asked him to become head gardener when he left the moor. 'I didn't know one flower from another, but I went. And I wouldn't start till 8.30am – I was sick of this 6 o'clock in the mornin' stuff. It was a big garden of ten acres and I was in charge of three others, but I didn't 'ave any real work to do. I only did it for a few months.

'After that the curator of the castle asked me to go on the gate taking the tickets. But I said, "You've got the wrong feller. I'm the one who shifts 'em out, not gets 'em in".'

Since then Newton has taken things at a much more leisurely pace. His wife Joyce died several years ago and he now lives alone, but he sees a lot of his son Brian and his four daughters. He also remains at the centre of the shooting grapevine.

Newton Hutchinson has clearly enjoyed his career, especially his time at Raby, where he has been very well looked after. 'My pay was never a ha'penny wrong. If I were a 14-year-old I'd do it all again.' And even now, given half a chance, I believe the man sitting quietly, puffing his pipe, would seize the opportunity to relive some of the old times. After all, his wardrobe still contains some of his heavy-tweed keeper's suits going back several decades. It's as if he is expecting to be called back into service at any moment.

A MATCH FOR ANY POACHER

GEORGE COLE

BERKSHIRE, DERBYSHIRE, HAMPSHIRE AND ANGLESEY

Any poacher who dared tackle George Cole in his prime inevitably came off worse because this renowned keeper was also an expert boxer. Indeed, in 1936 he was the sparring partner of Tommy Farr when the British champion fought Max Baer for the world title. This came about because both men trained at the Green Man on Blackheath. 'And 'e was bloody rough with his sparring partners too. But the first time I had a go I was still on me feet after three rounds. So we did the same the next day and after that I was given complimentary tickets for the big fight.'

At that time George was in the Metropolitan Police, but not surprisingly he 'could not stand being shut up in the town' and it was not long before he felt the need to get back into the keepering life, which was such a strong tradition in his family.

One of only two children, George Ernest Frederick Cole was born on 10 March 1916, at his maternal grandparents' house at Cookham in Berkshire, his father being away in the war. His paternal grandfather was headkeeper for thirty years up to retirement at the nearby Penn estate, where he headed a team of fourteen underkeepers, including George's father and three uncles. They wore bowler hats and velvet livery with brass buttons.

The first thing George can remember is, 'rolling around in grandad's churn. He kept dog biscuits in it and I was well and truly stuck so auntie had to get me out. Grandad had two kennels – one for flat-coats and another for curly-coated retrievers. I never liked the curlies as they bit.

George Cole's father 'at work' in the rearing field. Sadly, the boy with him was killed in the war

'Grandad fed the pheasants at Penn on a sort of stiff custard made from eggs and milk. The birds apparently thrived on it – and I should think the keepers had to let their suits out a bit at the end of the season.

'I also remember seeing newts in the well-water when we raised the lid, so that shows you how fresh it was.'

When George was three the family moved to Ambergate, in Derbyshire, where his father was underkeeper on the Belper estate. And when he was seven they moved to the Foremark estate [now Repton School], Derbyshire, where father became headkeeper.

'From Foremark I had about four miles to walk to school at Ticknall, but I didn't mind. On the way there I used to trap moles and skinned 'em as I went. I got a tanner [2½p] apiece for 'em. The estate also had a full-time mole catcher who worked for a farthing an acre.

'I liked school and even went to evening classes. I never missed   *and* we often had four-foot snowdrifts. It was always cold up there, but coal was cheap as we weren't far from the mines. The food was good too. I often went off to school with a bacon sandwich. But although I liked lessons I never saw any farther than goin' into keeping.'

George's earliest memories of shooting concern going along as 'stop' – a task traditionally given to responsible boys and old chaps no longer able to keep up with the beaters. 'Off we'd go at 7am to keep the birds in and often stayed put right into the afternoon, until they shot that covert. Damn cold too, but you could have a little fire. We got about half a crown each for that.

'The beaters got four shillings, a bottle of Burton beer and bully beef sandwiches: mother used to be up half the night makin' them from a yard-long loaf and a 40lb tin of Fray Bentos. We needed about thirty beaters then and on a shoot day there was always plenty turned up to see if there were any vacancies.'

George left school at the age of fourteen and went to work in the gardens at Sir Francis Burdett's Foremark Hall, knowing that a keepering vacancy was coming up. 'I was keeperin' for father anyway.

'In the garden I earned 7/6d a week. There were half a dozen of us, with three or four living in a bothy. There was a tremendous amount of mowing, but not for me – I just wheeled barrow loads of grass away. It seemed to be cold all the time there – except when you were digging.

'When I was fifteen I became keeper's boy, doin' anythin' that nobody else wanted to do. I got ten bob a week, of which I was allowed to keep half a crown. It was an enjoyable time. There was a lot more happiness in the countryside in those days and the communities stayed in the villages.

'One year, millions of starlings came into our larch plantation, where I had six- to seven-week-old pheasants. They ruined the wood with their droppings and breaking the branches, and there was a 2 to 3in runnin' mass underneath. We tried every way to shift 'em – hawk kites, sulphur fires and shooting – but it did no good and we had to abandon the wood. The birds eventually left in the spring and millions of elder trees came up under the roost, from the seeds in the berries they'd been eating.

'I had my first night-poaching case when I was seventeen. It was seven in the

evening and I was just settin' the alarm guns around the woods – you never set 'em early as the pheasants would trigger 'em going to roost – when three or four shots went off. I ran round to cut the culprits off and met two blokes with some pheasants and a .410. Then we had a bit of a set to and one man bent the gun barrel over me head. But I had this ash plant with a ferrule on the end and I hit him on the head with it, splitting the stick and my hand too. I had a go at the other one as well but in the end we had to give up and off they went.

'I had an idea who the men were and biked four miles to fetch the village policeman. When we went round one was at home but he denied it. However, the police found the .410 in his lavatory. They got the other man the next day. I went with the police to where he was working on a road gang, and when we lifted his cap there was the bloody great gash I gave him. Both men got two years inside.

'After the war I was playin' darts at a pub in Repton when I saw this chap and he took his cap off and said, "Just run your hand over this". It was the poacher I hit all that time ago and he still had a ridge in his skull to prove it.

'When I was nineteen, Major Betterton – the shoot leader – urged me to join the police, saying there was no future in keepering. So I did. But you had to be twenty to join the county force and I couldn't wait, so I went to the Metropolitan, who took you younger.

'I did a bit of everything. I was on the beat and out in the old Wolseley 25s – there were only a few cars then – and had a turn in the CID. Also I had to do a month's traffic duty in the Blackwall tunnel, but it was much

quieter in those days. The only trouble was the trams – they wouldn't stop for anybody because they were frightened they'd get stuck on the dead patch.

'There was nothing too vicious then: most people were satisfied with a decent punch-up. Just pop 'em in the old Black Maria and off to Blackheath. There was no real malice in those days. Anyone we run in we'd probably have a drink with the next night.'

After three years George longed for the green fields again and in 1938 went along

to Cruft's Dog Show, then recognised as the keepers' clearing house. 'It was good then because you really felt at home there. Anyway, I met Dickinson – the headkeeper at Somerley, near Ringwood in Hampshire, and was taken on as second keeper on the spot. There were five keepers at Lord Normanton's estate then.'

Somerley has long been renowned for the variety of wildfowl which visit the river there, as well as its pheasants. The duck have been shot using the old system

During the 1930s, George found time for some ferreting while on leave from the Metropolitan Police

of gazes [blinds] which enable the Guns to approach the river unseen. 'There were several miles of these along the river and two old pensioners spent the whole of every summer making them. They scythed the spear grass and threaded it between rails. It was a work of art. After the war there was not so much spear grass so I added birch.

'On a duck shoot I stood where all the Guns could see me drop a flag and start walking in together, so that everyone had a fair chance. We only shot it three or four times a year. In those days even the farm workers were not allowed to walk the meadows in case the duck were disturbed. A punt was used to pick up the shot birds, and that took some doing in a current of three or four knots. One old chap was so strong he always had dry elbows at the end of it. The bag was just under 500 a day in 1947. We also used to get lots of snipe and once killed seventy in an hour.'

Wildfowl shooting has always been George's favourite form of the sport. 'I've only ever shot one partridge in my life. I always thought it far too nice a bird. Whenever they wanted a brace or two for the house I used to send old Jack.'

There was no doubting George's marksmanship on claypigeons: in 1950 he won the Browning Cup at the New Forest Show. 'My wife had to walk down to the Post Office to draw out another £5 to pay for the cartridges I needed in the shoot-off. I was so pleased to beat all the semi-professionals, I took the cup home, filled it with whisky and had a good celebration.'

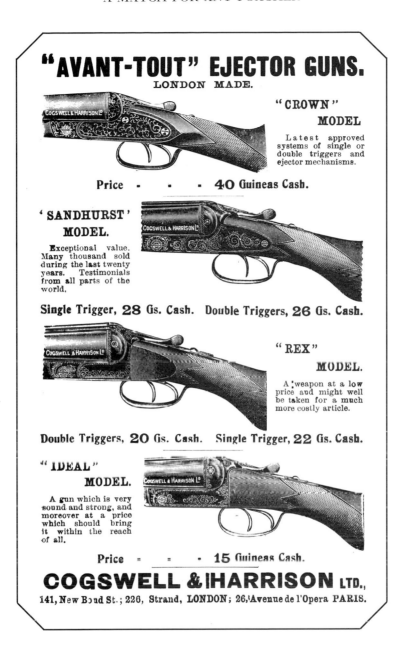

In 1939, the year before he married Marjorie at Repton, George joined the 26th Light Ack-ack Regiment at Tutbury, in Derbyshire. 'We never had a uniform – just walked about in an old rugby scarf and great coat and went rabbitin' in between goin' round the country. I was never much of a military chap – never liked polishin' stones.

'The best bit was when we were stationed at Hatfield. I always carried my 16-bore with me in the kitbag in case of a bit of a shoot. I often used to get hares, pheasants and wildfowl – with the permission of the farmers. After a while Captain Grierson heard about it and he wanted to join in too. He wasn't a military chap either. We were only part-time soldiers. Sometimes we got rabbits and all sorts of game and used to swap it.'

Then George joined the *Andes* troop carrier at Liverpool and went to Palestine, in the 3rd Field Regiment of the Royal Horse Artillery – 'only they had no horses then'. Here, too, he did a bit of gameshooting when he could, 'but I had trouble with the local cartridges in an old hammergun'.

His travels took him to South Africa too. 'Tobacco was only 3d an ounce there compared with about a shilling at home, so I came back with a sackful. Once I was never seen without me pipe. I smoked an ounce a day for forty years – even in the desert.

'I ended up with the 8th Indian Division – they were always in the thick of it. Those Indians didn't believe in coming out for a rest – they thought it was a waste of time as fresh troops would have to get used to the shells comin' over. Mind you, the Gurkhas were real medal hunters, though they were all gentlemen.

'When we were in Italy we washed and shaved in Champagne or some other wine – it was easier to get than water. I also went to Egypt and Turkey, and then, just when I was nicely settled back home I had to go to Germany, at the end of 1945. It was bloody cold there too after the heat of the desert.'

George left the Army in 1946, obviously without much regard for the medals he acquired. He turned the campaign stars into key rings, which he still uses. 'They give a nasty jab in the leg so there's not much chance of losing them.'

He did not intend to go back into keepering after the war. 'I thought it was too hard and I'd got used to having my nights off.' So he became a county land drainage officer, 'in charge of the prisoners as I could speak their language a bit. But we could not get the Italians to work, so I decided to put a Jerry in charge of 'em as the Germans were so efficient. That soon stopped 'em goin' round the shops and after the girls.'

Later that year George returned to Somerley, to work on the river for two years before becoming headkeeper. 'When I went back the gyppos had taken charge. The first lot I came across was two pickin' daffodils by the house, so I went straight up and challenged them – I was really fit then. I smacked the tall one straight in the midriff and he fell about 12ft onto the concrete support of the bridge. Then the little one ran off. I was really worried about the chap who'd fallen, but up 'e got and off he went.

One of six double-spring otter traps which George Cole had made to protect the trout hatchery at Somerley soon after the war

'Anyway, I thought I'd better go to see his lordship and tell him all about it in case anything came of it. I thought he might rollick me for being too rough, but instead he said, "Good – I'll pay the fine if there is one and you sort the rest of them out". So after that we really gave the gyppos a tough time.'

At that time the estate also suffered through a large number of otters going into the trout hatchery. 'It was easy meat for them', George remembers. 'So I had six Lane's double-spring, 6in spiked-jaw otter traps made. The ordinary ginns wouldn't hold the otter. I always remember old man Lane – he had a gold Albert across his chest and a little gold trap attached to it.

'One year we caught thirty-odd otters, but now I regret it. No one then would have dreamed that the otter would become so rare. Trapping them was perfectly legal then. The best one weighed over 30lb and their skins were worth £3 10s each.

'It was about that time the landlord of the Fish Inn – Johnny Frampton – used to come picking-up regularly. One day a hen pheasant got up and was wounded. Obviously we didn't want it to get away and were so insistent that a Gun shot at it dangerously before it disappeared into a withy bed. Unfortunately, Johnny poked his head round a stack but forgot how much his stomach stuck out, so he got peppered.'

Luckily Johnny wasn't badly hurt and this gave George the opportunity for a little fun, through making an unusual entry on the game card. As usual, Lord Normanton read out the bag at dinner that evening, '. . . pheasants and one Frampton. What's a Frampton?' Of course, this brought tremendous laughter, but George had warned Colonel Wright, one of the Guns, about the prank, so it was taken in the right spirit.

'That morning Johnny Frampton had also backed the horse Tent Peg, and won £100, so he ended up with gold and lead on the same day.' Johnny was obviously

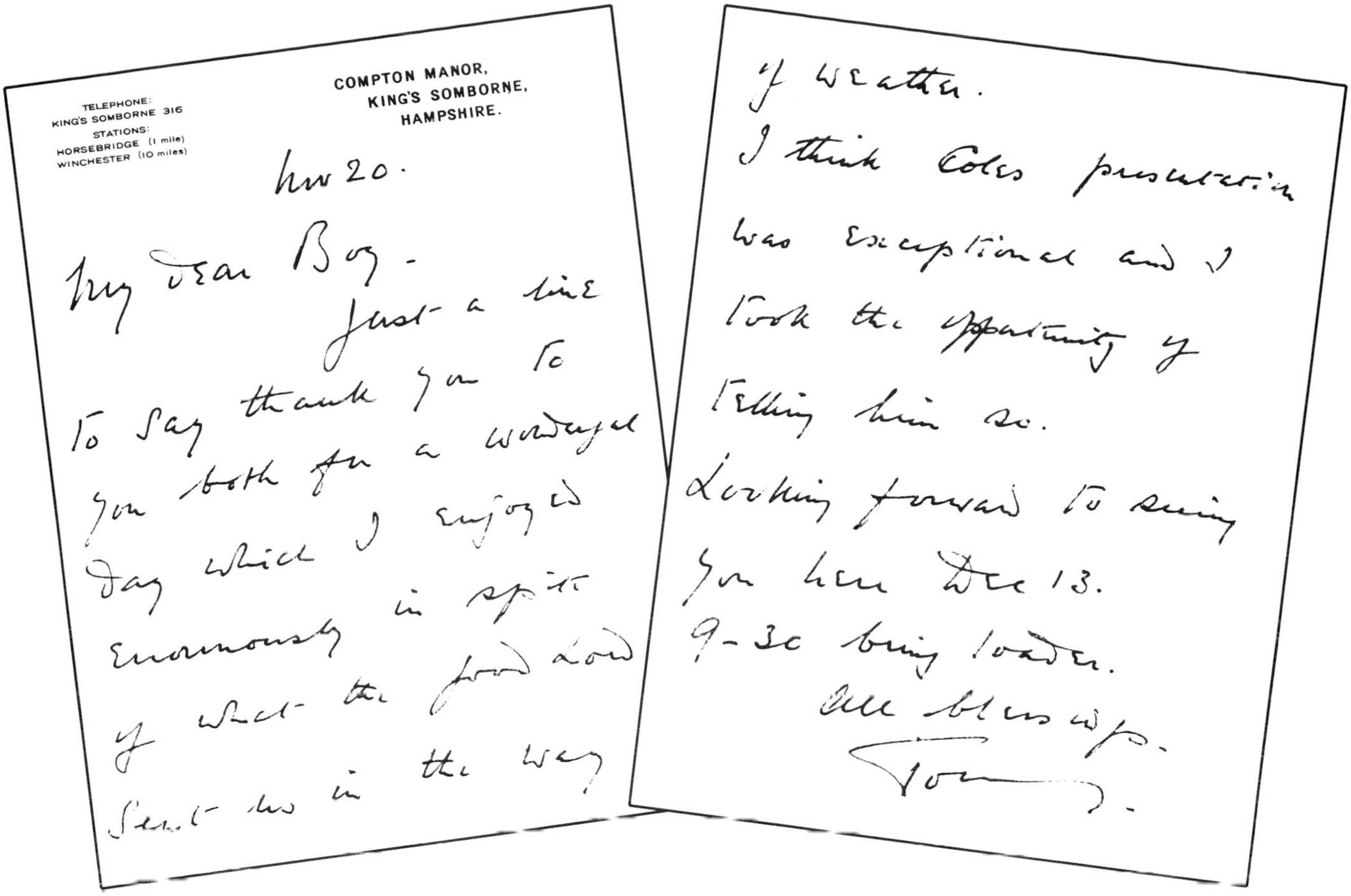

COMPTON MANOR,
KING'S SOMBORNE,
HAMPSHIRE.

TELEPHONE:
KING'S SOMBORNE 316
STATIONS:
HORSEBRIDGE (1 mile)
WINCHESTER (10 miles)

Nov 20.

My Dear Boy.

Just a line to say thank you to you both for a wonderful day which I enjoyed enormously in spite of what the *food lord* sent us in the way of weather.

I think Coles preservation was exceptional and I took the opportunity of telling him so.

Looking forward to seeing you here Dec 13. 9-30 being loaders.

All bless up.
Tommy.

(above) A letter of thanks to Lord Normanton ('Boy') and his keeper George Cole from the famous Tommy Sopwith of Compton Manor. (below) A letter of thanks from Reginald Dalrymple

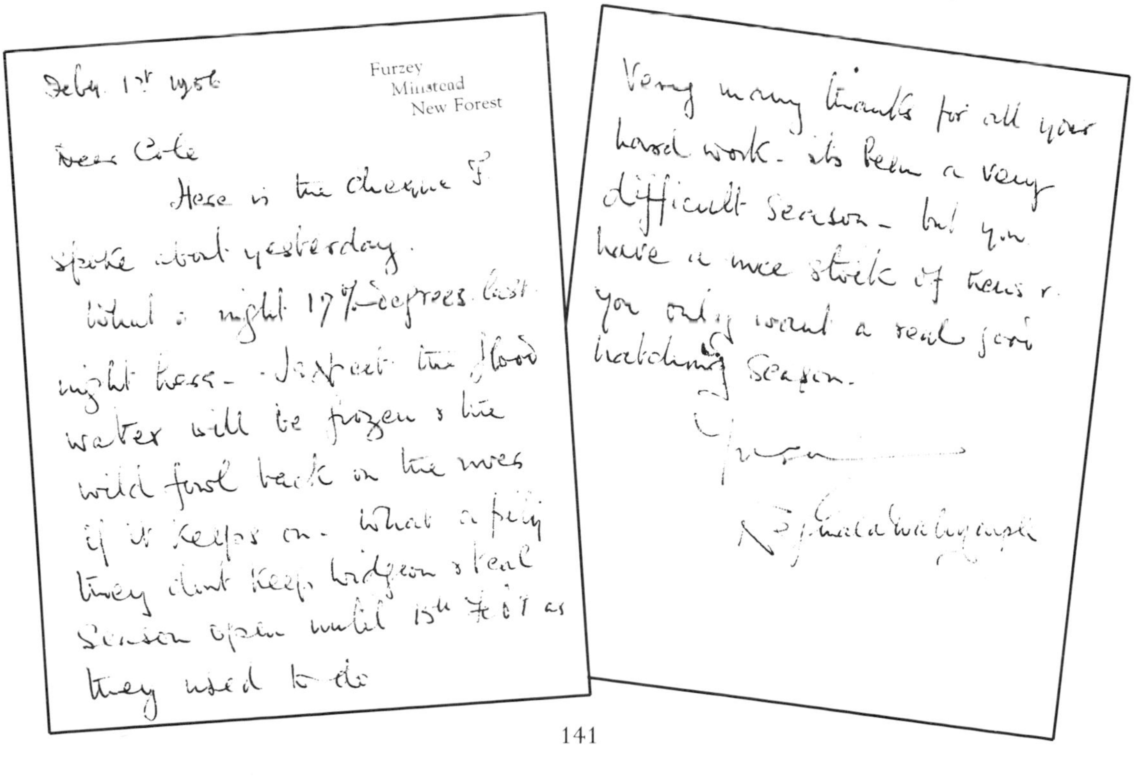

Feby 1st 1956

Furzey
Minstead
New Forest

Dear Cole

Here is the cheque I spoke about yesterday.

What a night 17° degrees last night here. Expect the flood water will be frozen & the wild fowl back on the moss if it keeps on. What a pity they don't keep widgeon & teal season open until 15th Feby as they used to do

Very many thanks for all your hard work. Its been a very difficult season - but you have a nice stock of birds & you only want a real good hatching season.

Yours
Reginald Dalrymple

delighted with the way things turned out and gave George an old bottle of whisky to commemorate the occasion. That treasured bottle still remains unopened in the Cole household.

On another occasion at Somerley it was George who was on the receiving end of a shot. 'I was out rabbitin' with old Jack Reed – a wartime keeper, when he accidentally peppered me from only five or six yards. Luckily I had a leather jacket on, but it was shredded and I had eighteen pellets in me back. I went to see the family doctor and he said, "Well, I'll squeeze a few out, but we'll never get the rest". So he did and off I went to the Fish. A few noggins cure most things. I always reckon the drink must have come out the holes in me back and cauterised 'em. Poor old Jack Reed was there, too, drowning his sorrows, but he'd thrown his gun away and said he'd never shoot again.'

In the early 1960s George found a mink's nest in a rabbit hole in a wood called the Dog Kennels. 'The authorities didn't believe it at first as it was one of the first in the country, and the story was on TV. The farm it escaped from offered £1 each animal, so I thought why bother – I might as well skin them myself. So I ended up selling them to the Hudson Bay Company, through London. When they were cured, matched up and auctioned they fetched a really good price – £12 to £18 a

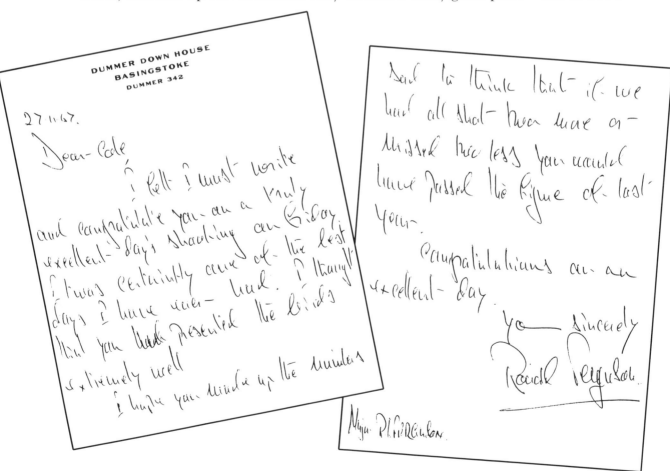

A letter of congratulation from Major Ronald Ferguson, father of Sarah, the future Duchess of York

skin. This went to two of the four underkeepers who picked 'em up in catch-'em-alive traps.'

George obviously had great affection for the late Lord Normanton – the fifth Earl. 'He often used to ring up for me just to go and have a chat in the kitchen. He had such a fund of wonderful stories and he was a good friend. One day I came across him by the river. I'd heard this *tick tick tick* and wondered what it was. He was sitting there peacefully with his feet in the water and his bike upside down, turning the pedals by hand. I said, "What's to do m'lord?" and he said, "It's much easier to sit here doing this than that damn exercise my wife wants". Apparently, whenever he returned home, Lady Normanton would look at his mileometer to check that he had done the required twelve miles to get his weight down. He also used to sneak off to smoke – always had Trumper's Silk Cut—handmade for him.'

The fifth Earl died in 1967 and in 1973 George decided to take a job as headkeeper for Sir George Meyrick at Bodorgan, Anglesey. He retired there at the age of sixty-five and in the same year received his CLA forty-year service medal from Prince Charles at the Bowood Game Fair. He and his wife still live on the estate, in a lodge along a delightfully quiet lane. George was succeeded as head by his son Walter. His other son – Willy – was a shooting instructor at the West London Shooting Ground, where he taught Henry Ford before going on to work for the motoring mogul. George also has three daughters, and their grandson Paul Ashton is a keeper at Lincolnholt, so the family tradition of keepering seems set to continue well into the future.

When George first went to Anglesey, 'old Jack Jones had keepered the estate for thirty years and said he'd never seen a fox! And they told me there were no foxes at all on Anglesey, but I shot one here within only a few weeks.

'At first I thought Anglesey were paradise – just like Somerley used to be, with hardly any traffic. But there were thousands and thousands of corvids and pigeons, and with all the crows and jackdaws sat round about every tree looked like it was covered with apples. So we set to work and cleared up all the rookeries. The trouble is a lot of farmers don't like to see 'em shot. There aren't many trees here – mostly only a few around the farmhouses, and the owners are superstitious enough to think that if the crows go the money goes too.'

However, George did not have too much trouble with 'two-legged vermin' on Anglesey. 'They're mainly fish poachers in Wales, and there are plenty of good places where the sea-trout run.'

Looking back on a very full life, George told me, 'I couldn't have picked a nicer set of employers.' In serving them he has

Headkeeper George watches his ex-boss, the late Lord Normanton (the fifth earl), collect a pheasant at Somerley

certainly met a few characters and celebrities and has witnessed some fine sport. 'Lord Eldon was the best Shot I ever saw. I was loading for him at Lord Cranborne's in Hampshire. Raoul Millais – the artist – could really shoot too. I loaded for him at Clarendon, where I once saw Lady Sopwith get forty birds at one stand. This was at the King Edward Belt and she really showed Tommy Sopwith and Lord Louis how to do it.'

But others were not always to be admired. 'There was old 110% Cobbold, the banker, who lined birds up before shooting. And Peter Playdel-Bouverie always shot two Guns' width either side of him: if he was in the middle of the line the whole lot would be in jeopardy. The boss always used to say, "Oh no!" if he drew the peg next to him.'

While at Somerley, George was a frequent visitor to nearby Broadlands, where his son Walter was second keeper to the famous Harry Grass. 'We didn't even dare tell dad that the Queen was coming', Walter told me. 'Anyway, he was picking up in Town Copse and at the end of it a woman shouted across, "I think we've finished here", so dad called back, "OK, we'll amble on up now". Imagine his surprise when he discovered it was the Queen.'

George was also picking up at Broadlands on the record day when Prince Philip laid his guns down on the grass because the barrels were too hot. 'He shot 200 at

one stand alone. In fact he, Lord Brabourne and Cunningham-Reid had 200 each at Town Copse. They shot 2,000 that day and in the evening I said to Grass I wouldn't like to open Lord Louis' post next morning when the antis get to hear about it. Well, Harry went and told this to his boss and afterwards he sent back the message, "Tell Cole he's bloody well right".

But despite all the tough times and having to deal with awkward people from all walks of life, George Cole remains one of the gentlest people you could wish to meet. A lifetime outdoors learning to live with nature has left him with a wonderful air of contentment.

THE LIKELY LAD

RON ANTHONY

HAMPSHIRE AND SUSSEX

'One day the agent for the estate, Captain S. Else, came into the school. There were five of us leaving and I suppose 'e 'ad a look round and saw I was the likeliest one for boy keeper. I said yes straightaway, and I started on 30 July 1934, on the Monday.'

Although he was not from a keepering family, it was not surprising that Ronald Anthony showed such promise, because even at the age of fourteen he was a countryman through and through. Born on Friday 13 August 1920, at the hamlet of Dean Lane End, Rowlands Castle, Hampshire ('the house was in Sussex and the garden in Hampshire'), he was the son of a self-employed copse underwood-cutter, hurdle-maker, sheep-shearer and thatcher.

'For boys in those days, as soon as you got useful you 'ad to 'elp father, so I started to shear sheep at the age of ten and by twelve I could manage the job fully. This was all hand shears too. I also helped with the copse cuttin' and makin' bunts – 3- to 4-ft-long bundles of brushwood to heat the ovens. A bunt was trimmed but a baffin was not. And there was faggots too. There was never a lot of money about then. We 'ad no choice. If you could work and earn some money you was a good boy.

'There was only the odd tractor about then. Father did a round of farms – seasonal work. He was in a gang of four with grandad, uncle and my brother. In winter, father and uncle used to supplement their income by goin' beatin' on shoots.

'At harvest time I drove the horse and wagon to the fields and ricks. There were three or four pairs of horses and lots of men on most farms. I remember one time, it was the last day of the harvest and I'd been workin' on this farm from haytime in June right through to the end of the corn in August. The farmer called me in and I was really rubbin' me hands, expecting about five bob, but he only gave me 1/6d.'

In those days farming was in the doldrums, but the Anthony family was better off than most other country folk. The Idsworth estate had started selling off properties after World War I and in 1919 Ron's father had taken the opportunity to buy his cottage and the adjoining one, 'where grandad lived. They cost £200 – all his savings, but there was about an acre of ground too. Farm workers' wages was only about thirty bob then, but as dad was self-employed he wanted to work all hours and got double that. All piece-work.

'All father 'ad was the bike, but grandad couldn't ride one so 'e 'ad a pony and trap as 'e was in his seventies then. But when 'e was a bit younger 'e used to walk to work from Chalton to near Chichester Barracks and back – twelve miles each way. He was shepherdin' then and 'e used to leave at two in the morning, running down the hills.

Outside the Red Lion, Chalton, in about 1905. Helping policeman Bob Wynne are Ron Anthony's grandfather (left), uncle (right) and father (unwrapping bread from a cloth). His auntie and uncle's wife are in the doorway. Note the old beer jugs and the wooden settle (left), used to support beer barrels. Beneath the trap door in the foreground was a big water tank

'In those days you sort of 'ad a love of workin' 'orses and if you could help 'em a bit you did. You never rode in the cart uphill – most of the time we'd give 'em a pull, with a rope over the shoulder and secured to the step iron.'

From the age of eight, Ron started to help on shoots. 'I went as stop and got half a crown on Idsworth and three shillings at Stansted. Sometimes I walked three miles to get there. It was always cold standin' around and sometimes you was unlucky enough to get a drive not shot till half past three. But you lit a fire – in fact they liked it as you kept movin' about to get the sticks and movement is essential to keep the birds in. There'd be six to twelve boys, plus a dozen beaters who got six shillings each.

'We always took our own food in those days, but during the Second World War Idsworth provided a lot of stew as there was thousands of rabbits. We 'ad a lot of sailors come beating then and they was all useless. They went through a wood like a load of ducks – one behind the other, takin' the easiest path. But they loved that stew and always came round with their plates a second or third time.'

Like so many lads, Ron started shooting with an airgun. Then he graduated to a No. 1 garden gun firing 7mm Saloon cartridges, and some solid ball. 'We shot the usual sparrows and took pot-shots at anythin' we could get away with. There

was an old cowl on the house and that 'ad a few holes in it. Later on I 'ad a 20-bore and I thought I was really well armed, but cartridges were hard to come by and dished out like sweets, a few at a time.'

So it was an experienced Master Anthony who, at fourteen years old, joined the team of four keepers at Idsworth. The estate was owned by Major A. F. Clarke-Jervoise JP DL, who let the shooting to Lorna, Countess Howe. Ron's pay was twelve shillings for a seven-day week, 'hours according to the season. As boy keeper I 'ad all the nasty jobs, such as cleanin' out the ferrets and taking out the muck when the broodies was off – for about twenty minutes for feeding and watering every morning. I carried the birds' corn round in a side bag, and sometimes took a ½cwt sack too.

'The broodies were tethered in groups of four, which shared a water dish in the middle, but they each had their own 'andful of corn next to their stick.

As a lad, Ron was proficient in sheep-shearing as well as many other country skills

Broodies, the backbone of old-time pheasant rearing

The 'stop' could build a fire

'After two years at that father decided to take me away to learn his trade and I spent another two years becoming fully proficient in hurdle-making etc, as well as experienced with working horses – from ponies to the heavy shires.

'But I didn't like it as I already 'ad the taste for keeperin', so as soon as a job came up, in 1938, for a single keeper at Idsworth I took it. There was no cottage and I got £1 a week, 10s of which I gave to mother. I cycled a mile or two to work each day and worked for a syndicate on the Sussex side of the estate.'

Ron had hardly settled into the job when war loomed. 'In 1939 I was becomin' twenty in the August and would be up for conscription, so in April 1940 I went and joined the Marines while I still 'ad the choice. We started at Deal, but there was so many air raids it interfered with our trainin' so they sent us to Chatham for a year. Then it was back to Portsmouth and soon on to HMS *Berwick*. We went to Iceland and the Denmark Straits, shadowin' convoys to Russia for two years. I was also on the *Indefatigable* aircraft carrier.

'I was invalided out with arthritis in 1944. I suppose it was through being exposed to the elements on the upper deck anti-aircraft gun. All we 'ad was a duffle-coat – no proper waterproofs then. I also had an operation for kidney stones on the *Berwick*. I'd signed on for twelve years but I never liked the water.'

In October 1944 Ron returned to Idsworth, to the Huckswood beat. 'Food was

still rationed after the war but we started to rear pheasants in 1946, using ground-up dog biscuits and some wangled eggs – one day the agent arrived with twenty-four dozen. And there was always plenty of rabbits to chop up. But it was a struggle to rear and we only did it every other season for a few years. But the place was very well keepered and 1947 was an exceptionally good season, when we shot 1,400 pheasants. And I always remember the winter of 1947–8 because of an ice storm which froze the rain on the trees, so that when the pheasants went off roost some left their tails stuck to the branches.'

With the Major's connections and many naval bases nearby, the shoot had a distinctly nautical flavour. Entries in Ron's gamebook reveal that there were no less than five admirals – Dawnay, Layton, Grantham, Edelstone and Bonham-Carter – plus three captains – Weir, Phillips and Holcroft – at one shoot. 'We had a lot of ex-commanders-in-chief of Portsmouth. They always spoke their mind, and when one day Bishop Fleming of Portsmouth shot a fox 'e never lived it down. The Bishop usually came on Boxing Day. We also had the Lord Mayor of Portsmouth out.

'But the Major didn't shoot. For him lunch was the highlight of the day – always at 1pm prompt. He was a stickler for time, even though it was never easy to plan things just so. And if 'e couldn't stop for tea at four 'e was most disgruntled. He used to like lordin' it about with his chauffeur in 'is Packard shooting brake and Rolls, with his pennant flying because 'e was High Sheriff. Although he 'ad a gun an Avant Tout – he usually gave it to the chauffeur to use. Fishing was his main interest. He was a very superstitious chap who didn't like green and hated the number thirteen, but 'e died on Friday the 13th – just fell back in bed, aged ninety-three in the '70s.'

Ron married Vera in 1944. 'She's a townee, from Portsmouth, evacuated to Finchdean, where I met her workin' in the pub. She used to help with the meals at the big house, and one day the Major said to her, "Are your knees cold?", which was his way of sayin' he thought her skirt was too short.

'He was a bit of an actor and comedian too and would perform at Stansted estate, where they had their own theatre, as well as sing ditties and play the piano at the harvest suppers we 'ad just after the war. They killed a bullock for the first one in 1946, and it was lovely to see a plate of meat then with the rationing still on.

'With the Major's housekeeper everythin' 'ad to be just so. They had some fine lunches there, with the port passed more than once, and everybody always came back out on form. An awful lot of butlers came and went and the housekeeper always sent for me when there was any trouble because I was a special constable.

'One time she called me and the bricklayer up to escort the butler off the place because 'e was so drunk. He'd locked 'imself in his room so the bricklayer went to get 'is club hammer, but the butler opened up before he returned. We got 'im down to Rowlands Castle station but he was in no fit state. His case was full of empty bottles – the Major's I suppose – and we kept findin' empty glasses all over the place when he'd gone.'

Ron's position as special constable was especially helpful in a heavily poached area because this gave him the same powers as a full-time police officer. 'It used to shake 'em rigid when I showed 'em my warrant card and seized their tackle. They

A party of fox shooters in Middle Park, near Havant, soon after the war. Left to right: headkeeper Wolfries from Stansted Park; C. Miles (chauffeur for Major Clarke-Jervoise); Walter Mason (farmer); Walter Cresswell (beatkeeper at Idsworth); anon; Charlie Royal (local baker); Sam Sadler (beatkeeper at Stansted); anon; anon; anon; Mr Gates (Havant auctioneer); Charlie Masters (beatkeeper at Idsworth); Charles Whitlock (headkeeper to Sir Dymock White). Ron Anthony missed the day because he injured his knee playing cricket

Ever watchful: Ron always carried a gun for vermin control

was always comin' out from the town in their cars and vans – and even lorries.

'But there was one time in August 1956 you didn't have to be very intelligent to spot somethin' was goin' on – a London taxi drivin' around the countryside at 6am is pretty conspicuous! It was two taxi drivers from a holiday camp at Hayling Island and they come several times before I caught 'em. When I stopped the taxi they claimed they were picking horse mushrooms! They were each fined £2 for trespassing in search of game, £3 for taking game without a licence, 10s for killing game out of season and £2 for a breach of the Poaching Prevention Act. Their two .410 shotguns were confiscated and sold in the market at Petersfield, the funds going to the county treasurer. The funny thing is they 'ad to buy one back as they'd borrowed it from a man at Hayling.

'Another time there was a man and wife on the land and I challenged 'em. She

'ad a handbag with a ferret in and they'd been catchin' rabbits. But when I reached for the bag she screamed and he threatened me as she was a bit pregnant. But as soon as I came back with a bobby she handed the bag straight over.

'PC William Robert Trent always looked after us and we made sure 'e always 'ad some shooting. He was the best country bobby I've ever had the privilege to know, especially regarding his expert knowledge of the Game Laws and anythin' to do with gypsies. We were out many nights together, which tied in well with the chicken patrols at Christmas. We went out in an unmarked estate van and the Major never minded me helping the police as he was a magistrate.

'Gypsies used to come round at any time of the year which suited them best and camp in their regular places such as Wick Bottom, Boscombe Bottom, Netherley, Railway Arch, Lay Piece, Dean Lane End, and Woodcroft by the railway – to name but a few. Of course, they were a great nuisance to keepers, so whenever we could we moved 'em on, which wasn't easy; nor did they take kindly to it.

'My first mistake was to try and move a lot on unaccompanied. They gave me a lot of verbal abuse and then they started roughing me up, and they all pitched into me – two men, a woman and two little kids. It was bad enough trying to fight off two men, but then the woman attacked me from the rear, giving me a hefty kick up the bum, and followed that up with a blow on the back of the head, using the heel of a shoe in her hand. By Jove! was she vicious! Talk about Hell hath no fury like a woman scorned. Even the little kids, who must have been under five, put their two pennyworth in with sticks. All in all, I had a rough house, as you might say, and didn't visit any more gypsy camps on my own.

'Another time, there was a different lot not going to move for anybody, not even the "King's man" – the local policeman, even though I was very civil towards them. But they didn't reckon on PC Trent. So off I went to get him. As soon as he saw me he said, "Got a bit of bother mate?" I said, "Yes, a lot of bloody diddy's up Wick Bottom, ain't goin' to move". "Ain't goin' to move?" 'e says, "we'll soon see about that".

'So off we goes the two miles to Wick Bottom and approached with some caution as it was not unknown to be shot at with a catapult. Anyway, PC Trent sauntered into the camp and said to the oldest-lookin' male, "Ain't goin' to move I hear". And no more was said when he went towards the fire and started to kick hot embers into the tent, which was supported by benders. Believe me you never saw a tent and benders dismantled with such speed. Eventually they packed up, shut in the horses and went away down the road hurling abuse until they were out of earshot.

'The traditional gypsy tent had a board ridge 4in × 1in, of a length to determine the size of the tent. Holes were drilled in the board to stick the ends of the hazel-rod benders in, while the other ends went into the ground. The benders were cut from the copse or hedgerow, wherever they could find them. They were covered with a sailcloth or waterproof sheet and secured with meat skewers. The height of the tent was about three or four feet.

'The leisurely way PC Trent sauntered into the camp was remarkable, but then he rarely moved in excess of two miles per hour. That was the speed a constable was required to proceed at on foot by the Hampshire Constabulary.

Major Clarke-Jervoise (with scarf) with the Idsworth beaters in the 1950s

'Trent's advice to me was if I got roughed up again, I was to get in close to 'em quick and, "stamp on their bloody foot with them big, heavy boots you got on". They were damn heavy too, horsehide and nailed, made in Scotland by Hogg's of Fife, costing 33/6d in 1934.'

In 1954 Ron became headkeeper over three at Idsworth, where he remained until 1963, when the estate was sold and the shoot broken up. But someone of his calibre is never out of work long and he soon found a similar position at the nearby Buriton House estate, owned by Major Hugh Rose.

It was at Buriton that Ron was nearly killed. 'One night I spotted some people in a field using their car headlights to shoot rabbits. I approached along the road, which was sunk down, and climbed the bank to get a better look. As I peeped over the top this car was comin' straight towards me and as I blinked at the lights and ducked instinctively some pellets hit me. There was one in my nose, which is still there, and a couple more above my ear – you can still feel them under the skin. But fortunately they missed my eyes. This chap said 'e thought I was a hare! I didn't get anything for it, only a lot of abuse from the man's mother! Nothing was done about it as it turned out they had permission to be there and I hadn't been informed.'

Ron's father, too, was accidentally shot, by Charlie Curzon – the brother of Countess Howe – in 1932. 'Curzon shot at this low partridge. He was the end Gun and dad was the end beater. Just one pellet went through the boxcloth gaiter into

his leg and 'e shouted out immediately. Curzon apologised of course and gave dad a two bob bit, which was a good drink then and would buy 3oz of baccy. So dad said, "Next time I go 'e can shoot me again for two shillings".

'Also my son was shot when he was beating. Somebody 'ad a go at a hare on a pheasant shoot and a pellet went through his cheek. They took it out from the inside and 'e got £10 for that, but it was mostly to make up for his loss of a day's pay.'

This latter incident was at Leydene, Clanfield, where Ron went to work in 1971 after the Buriton shoot was broken up. He remained there – as a beatkeeper because the head forester was also designated headkeeper – for the remainder of his career. His boss was Sir Lynton White, whose family started the Timothy White's chain.

At Leydene Ron continued to take a traditionally tough line with foxes. 'You 'ad to keep right on top of 'em because if you let 'em lay on you during the winter then they'll cub down. I never 'ad any trouble because I kept thirty or forty snares goin' all year round, but before the fifties it always used to be a dead cat and a ginn, when that was legal.

'At night a peewit would always tell you when a fox was around. If one called I'd lean out the bedroom window and listen. Then I'd squeak 'im up and shoot 'im without even getting dressed. But the fox has a funny way of makin' sound

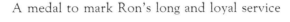

A medal to mark Ron's long and loyal service

seem very near and once I was lured up the road in my pyjamas. I must have looked a sight in the moonlight with gun in hand.'

Ron received his long-service medal at the Broadlands Game Fair in 1984 and retired in 1985 after fifty years as a keeper. But he has remained very active, especially in loading on various estates. Inevitably, this brings an endless round of entertainment, not least being the time just three years ago, 'when an old chap of eighty-five leaned back so far in stretching for a bird he fell on top of me'. But now Ron could do with rather less excitement as he has had a little heart trouble.

At his town home in Horndean, Hampshire, Ron still has many bits and pieces to remind him of a very full keepering life – from simple lists of beaters' pay to field trial cards from the forties and fifties, when he often acted as steward of the beat. But none is more interesting than the list at the back of his old gamebook, which records the everyday things which a keeper of his generation needed to purchase. The extracts below provide a fascinating insight into the 1950s. They echo the days when the honesty and loyalty of stalwarts such as Ron Anthony were unquestioned.

EXTRACTS FROM GAMEBOOK

1954

Feb   2   75 .410 cartridges @ 9/7 per 25 – £1 8s 9d

        8   5cwt of wheat 2nds from B. Bussell Esq @ 28/- per cwt

      10   Returned 200 ex-Govt. cartridges @ 35/- per 100 for 200
            Universal @ 49/- per 100

April 14   28lb fine grit 5/-
           56lb medium grit 10/-
           56lb limestone 7/6d
           2 doz nets 12/9d a doz
           1 gross snares £1 3s 9d

      20   2 doz china eggs 12/-
           3 doz brass rings 2/6d
           1 ball of cord 4/3d

      26   1 bottle poison £1 2s 6d

      27   300 rook cartridges from HAEC £3 15s

May   5   2cwt dog food from Lowe's @ 87/- per cwt

        6   300 eggs from Ashford, Kent @ £12 10s per 100
           1 tin cod liver oil 21/-

      15   68 broody hens @ 15/- each + 2 £51

      22   30 yds 3ft 1-inch mesh from Streets £1 10s 11d
           1 bottle tincture of steel, 1 tin insect powder 3/8d
           1 coil of binding wire 1/2d

June 6   1 pair prismatic binoculars from Flemmings £8 15s

      15   ½ gall BWD mixture 15/4d
           ½ gall Gapina 15/4d
           1 tin of Cardiac 9/6d

      23   1 round trap, 1 ride net from Young's Somerset £1 5s 6d

      29   1 scythe blade from Barbours 15/8d

July 10   3 sacks of corn from J. Budden Chalton £9 5s

Aug   4   10½cwt wheat from Home Farm @ 25/- per cwt £12 10s

        5   Game licences drawn £6

Sep   4   1 pair reflectors for van 4/6d

        6   2lbs powder, 200 caps, ½lb felt wads, 10lbs shot £3 5s 0d

Oct   24   50 12-bore cartridges lent to Capt Bonham-Carter

      26   1 doz 2½d stamps

Dec 23   1 puncture mended and patches and solution from Barratt's 6/5d

1955

Feb   7   expenses at Cruft's Show £1

Mar   7   4/9d and 3/9d for telegrams to Coventry and Totnes
           6 dog troughs and 2 whistles £2 4s 3d

Apr   7   30 earthenware feeding saucers £1 3s 9d
           2 doz snares, 2 doz rabbit traps, 3 Imbra traps £10 0s 6d

May	2	10/- for gun licence for Seal
	10	1 brass jag, 1 wire brush 12-bore from Havant Sports Services 6/1d
June	3	100 nitre chalk bags @ 2d each 16/8d
	7	1 padlock 4/9d
July	21	10 bottles TCP £1 15s 5d
Sep	24	keeper's hat purchased from W. Powell @ £10
Oct	14	3 loads of barley rakings from J. Budden 50/-
Nov	24	4 doz ales, 2 doz pint browns, 1 doz pint lights, 2 doz small browns, 6 lemons from George Inn

1956

Mar	16	15/6d for bed and breakfast at Fordingbridge
May	2	4 tins of Cymag @ 10/- per tin
	24	2 milk churns 5/- each
Oct	5	2 tins Rodine 7/- each
Nov	3	800 cartridges from Hercules @ 37/6d per 100

1957

Feb	11	£7 10s paid in cartridge rebate
Mar	6	1 spade handle 6/6d
Apr	3	135 Eley Gastight 28-bore £2
	13	1 petrol cap 5/-
May	13	1 driving mirror 5/8d
July	24	500 clay pigeons @ 2d each £4 3s 4d West Sussex Gun Club
Aug	31	Replacement Ford 8 engine (Barratt's) £29 10s
Sep	14	Anchor Stop clay trap Russell Hillsdons 19/10d
Dec	7	6 dozen fox wires (Youngs) £2 14s

1958

Jan	10	1 broom head 4/6d (Needhams)
Feb	8	£4 10s for Warfarin rat bait
July	17	3 suits £28 10s each (Privett's of Petersfield)

1959

Jan	16	10/- for advert in *Gamekeeper*
Feb	23	game register James & Co 16/-
April	4	£1 for beaters (rabbits) – 10/- Victor, 5/- John, 5/- Bill Martin
May	20	£1 for ferret doe £1 11s 6d gun repairs Smythe 1327

ON THE EDGE OF PARADISE

DON FORD

DORSET, HAMPSHIRE AND SUSSEX

It was entirely appropriate that Donald Walter Ford arrived in this world on the edge of a place called Paradise Wood, for he found life there almost idyllic. Born just three days before Christmas 1926, at Stourpaine, near Blandford in Dorset, he revelled in the unspoilt countryside. But perhaps that is not so surprising considering the fact his father, grandfather, great-grandfather and great-great-grandfather were all keepers before him, on Lord Portman's estate.

Don was out with his father from the word go, helping with tasks such as setting ginns, almost before he could walk. 'I used to traipse miles with father around his tunnel traps even before I went to school at the age of five. It was a wonderful place, with skylarks everywhere going up and down, and on the land it was all horses, with lots of downland, ploughin', drillin' and harrowin'. Dog roses and fruits covered the hedges, which were all overgrown – ideal for game but a nightmare for vermin control. We used to hang up stoats and everything else on a gibbet so that the boss could see the keeper was doin' his job. They made an awful smell. Everywhere you went there was a terrific lot of skeletons on the bushes, from a weasel to a black-backed gull.

'The rearing field was all broody hens of course, with just a few boughs for the young to run into for safety. But there was always a loaded gun by the hut in case a hawk came in, and plenty of time to deal with it as it sat on its kill.

'At night I helped father make snares, using a piece of wood with two nails and wire bought by the pound. Six-strand wire was OK for most work, but on hills 8lb was necessary because the rabbits runnin' down would thump it so hard. To braid it we put the wire through a meat skewer and then through the handle of a flat iron, which was given a good twist.

'We ran up to 300 snares and they had to be just right. Night-time I went with father to hold the torch, but sometimes mum wouldn't allow it when there was school next day. I also ran my own little line of twelve to fifteen snares, which I went to in the morning before going to school. A taxi used to fetch us at eight because we were

Don Ford's father

isolated, over five miles from Wareham. Some of the rabbits were sold and some fed to the dogs or pheasants after being chopped and ground up.

'I was mad on longnetting too. I got a real dab hand at that. I still have 100yds of net bought from Young's at Misserden in 1947. We used a lot of it when we kept rabbits breeding semi-wild. They kept the grass down, gave some food and a little money.

'Whole gangs went out at night. A couple of us held the net while the others walked round and grunted or sumat to make the rabbits run as fast as possible. But you had to be quick as we'd get eight or so at once.'

Don also helped with shooting many hundreds of rabbits. 'I had my first shot, with a .410, when I was four. I remember it well because it was a Sunday, when mum never worked because she was the daughter of a Methodist preacher and quite religious. We were on the lawn and father stood an apricot can on a post. He put just one 2in cartridge in the side-by-side hammergun, pulled the hammer back and passed me the gun. Off it went and the first thing I did was run over and see how many holes were in the tin. Years later, I did the same thing with my sons and grandson at four years old.

'Father used that gun for a lot of rattin' and rabbit-ferretin'. One day he had a lucky escape. He put the gun down and went to a bank. Meanwhile, the man on

the other side of the hedge fired and some of the shot went into the stock. It was still there when I sold the gun years later.

'When I was about ten I used to crawl miles with that .410, peepin' over banks after rabbits. And sometimes I'd walk up and jump out so that I could shoot 'em runnin'. I shot my first runner when I was seven.

'But there was a lot of wildfowl round too and I used to moan that I couldn't get 'em, even with the long cartridge. So when I was twelve I bought my first 12-bore. A friend with a sports shop brought out a single and a double and I chose the double Westley Richards. I put down a few quid and paid father back the rest – or most of it anyway.

'We used to poke sheets of paper soaked with Renardine down the rabbit holes for a couple of days and that made the rabbits sit out in the bushes. Then a shoot day would be a hell of a session. It was always a Saturday as that meant some of the farm workers could come too. One time I shot my first woodcock, and my arm was black and blue because I shot all day, but I wouldn't say it was too long. I must have fired 100 and some odd cartridges that day. All this made up my mind that keepering would be the life for me.'

Don certainly had plenty of opportunity to check that he was truly suited to the life. When he was twelve, his father was bedridden with sciatica and Don had to take over for a fortnight. 'We still had some of the old coops and it was very hard work, but I enjoyed it. You had to be very careful with mixing the food. If there was too much and some was left and the sun got on it then the birds soon got scour. After the fortnight father was really pleased.'

When the family was at Winterborne Tomson, Don went to Almer School (now

An old postcard of Dorset Guns and their bag, including a deer

a keeper's house), near Blandford, where his father was a single-handed keeper. 'From there we moved to Arne, near Wareham, where dad was head. Then I went to Stouborough School and on to Wareham Senior. When I was fourteen, the family moved to Kingston, near Corfe Castle, and I went as trainee on the Encombe estate, where father was head. I worked for Sir Ernest Scott for sixteen shillings a week. And as junior I had all the "best" jobs – feedin' the dogs, taking the horse and cart round for the rabbits, as well as rearing and caring for the ferrets.'

During the war, Don's father was in the Home Guard and the shoot often had combined rabbit/pheasant days, but all the birds were wild as no feeding was allowed.

When he was seventeen, Don volunteered for the Army, 'because they brought in the Bevan boys and I didn't want to go down the mines. Luckily, they didn't query my age, not being eighteen. I trained for six weeks at Colchester, then Norfolk, where I reckon I walked the whole of the county practising to be an infantryman in the Dorset Regiment. And I was very soon picked out for rifle shooting. The sergeant said, "You shoot some of those bloody Germans who shot my brother".' But Don never had the opportunity. Although he was posted to Gibraltar and Berlin, he was still in training on VE Day.

However, Don did have plenty of opportunity for sporting shooting during the war years. 'I always remember the night they bombed Coventry. I'd shot an Army haversackful of teal and on the way home was dodgin' the shrapnel. You could see all the planes as clear as anythin' in the moonlight.'

Fortunately, the family came through the war unscathed. 'The house we had been in at Arne was bombed and flattened, along with the kennels, because they had the ack-ack guns there. Another keeper lived there at the time, but luckily he wasn't in when Gerry called.'

After the war it was back to Encombe for two years. Then Don worked for three

years as a beatkeeper for Major David Wills, on the Lichfield Manor estate, near Newbury. This was followed by eighteen months on Sir Anthony Tichborne's estate, near Alresford, Hampshire. At the age of twenty-six he went to Sussex, to run a syndicate for Jack Aylwood, who took over from Sir Tom Sopwith. Don really enjoyed it there, but decided to leave in 1974 after twenty-two years when Aylwood died of cancer. He went to Lord Shaftesbury's Dorset estate at picturesque Wimborne St Giles, retiring as headkeeper at the age of sixty-five after seeing the 1991–2 season through. He is one of the few lucky keepers in recent years who have been given retirement homes on the estates they have served.

Much of Don's life has been spent controlling predators of game ('vermin'), but

in the old days he was allowed to use poisons as well as a whole arsenal of vicious traps. 'Strychnine was the best, especially in a half-buried rabbit for foxes. Then there was arsenic and, later on, zinc phosphide and Rodine for rats. We used to get a rabbit, slit it open and put Rodine on the liver – this was deadly for crows, which also came to the egg tray, a shelf 7–8ft up against a tree. Owls and other birds of prey were taken in pole traps. It's all illegal now, of course, which makes keeperin' so much harder.

'I caught my first fox at the age of twelve, to a pig which I found buried in a clump of trees, in a 6in grave. The foxes had already been there and eaten into it, so it was all smelly and falling to pieces. So I put some traps there, the big 6in badger ginns. Later I went back, but there was nothing there. I told dad and when he went there was a lovely fox with a white tip to its tail. I was really disappointed that I was the one to catch it but not kill it. Anyway, I skinned it out and sent it to Gordon's to be made up for mother for fox fur round the neck. But when it came back there was no white tip. So I wrote up and they said it was the right skin but the wrong tail as something was wrong with it, and it would cost me another ten shillings!

'Sometimes we used to half-bury a cat on a mound which foxes liked to roll on and do their business. One place I had six traps and the first night I caught a vixen,

Don with two badgers

169

which I skinned there and then, rolled the carcass on top of the mound and part covered it. Then I had nine more foxes in eleven days. When I was watchin' and could see the round shape of the mound I knew all was OK, but when I saw Charlie's silhouette dancin' around it was straight out with the gun.

'You can't beat a few spots of hare blood around your tunnel traps – brilliant! Then, if there's a stoat or weasel in the area you've got it. If you catch a rat or a stoat and get a bit of blood on the trap pan, next mornin' you always catch again. That's because they think it's been used by another and it's OK.'

But what Don regards as the most destructive of all predators is relatively new to the British countryside, having escaped from fur farms to establish feral populations in most areas. 'The mink

The mink

is the worst vermin of all. It can swim, jump, run and climb and has no enemy here except the human.

'The first time I had trouble with mink was back in 1964, when I had three dozen point-of-lay pullets in a pen. One morning I went to feed them and there was blood all over the snow and two or three birds dead in the pen. I dashed in the hut and there was a big pile of dead pullets, some with their heads off, and one or two barely alive. Immediately I thought it was the work of a ferret, grabbed an armful of traps and went to put one by a hole. But then I saw whiskers – he was still in there! So I went back and got the gun, gave a squeak, out came his head, and bang! He was really big – I couldn't get my hand round his neck. And the smell!

'Then I thought I'd get lots of money for the skin and sent it up to Horace Friend. But he said it was useless as it was wild and I got nothing. However, in later years they started taking 'em and I got up to £3 a skin.

'The mink will do no end of damage in the release pen. Once in Sussex I picked up 109 nine-week-old poults killed by one animal. You could tell it was a mink by the two little needle marks on top of the head. This devil only ate one bird, leaving the wings, head and gizzard, but some were part buried. Anyway, I already had twenty-two tunnel traps in the area, so I put more traps all over the place, some in tree stumps baited with turkey innards I got from Petersfield. But the mink didn't come for three nights. Then he climbed in, killed more birds and dug his way out. After that he left off for ten days and didn't go to any of the baits or tunnel

traps. Sometimes after he'd been there were birds part live next morning. He used to kill birds which were roosting up in the old man's beard and I never did catch him.

'But I've had some good experiences with vermin. I always remember one evening in Sussex in the fir plantation when I heard this crow shouting – he'd probably lost his mate or was lookin' for one. I called to him and he waited, then answered. Then I repeated it and he answered again. After that I started to change the call and he did too, going on copying each other for half an hour. Eventually he got bolder and came on and pitched up in the tree right above me, where I watched him and 'e made all sorts of antics. Then bang! and he was on the ground.'

One of Don's most unexpected catches was two badger cubs trapped by their feet in a ginn. 'I took them home, put Vaseline on their feet and reared them in a shed with turf on the concrete floor. Later I sold them to Ferndown Zoological Gardens.

'We used to get a lot of sparrowhawks here in Dorset, but no buzzards. Now there are loads of buzzards but they only kill a few birds in the release pen. The worst thing used to be the way the buzzard scared the pheasants from the fields into the woods, but now there are so many the pheasants don't take any notice. We always reckoned the best place for a buzzard was on the boundary, to keep our birds from strayin'.'

Like so many keepers, Don has lost a lot of game to poachers as well as predators. 'Sundays have always been bad as the casual poachers go round the roads with their catapults and air rifles. And a lot of gyppos take hares and deer. Now there are night patrols all the time. This shoot would be nothing without that. Some of these gyppos knew this land way back when they grew mangolds here, so they know it even better than me. Now they live in council houses and even own their own homes. Some say they bought them on the proceeds of poachin', just to annoy you.'

Back in Sussex, Don used an age-old method to frighten off both poachers and foxes. But his were not any old scarecrows. Indeed, 'people used to say how well-dressed they were. The body was wire netting, the head a paper bag, and they wore rubber boots, a hat and an old suit. Each one carried a lantern – a gallon petrol can with one side cut out, a 2lb jamjar inside with a night light top and a long wick. I filled it up weekly. The whole thing swivelled and flashed and the more you looked at it in the gloom the more you was convinced it was comin' towards you. We had them up every ride and they scared off lots of intruders.'

Once, however, it was Don who was surprised by a scarecrow. 'I was putting some birds to wood, and the night before I was getting the scarecrows ready. I was marchin' along with one under each arm when suddenly I felt something round the back of my neck. It was a dormouse which had its nest in the head of a dummy. Anyway, I caught it and put it in this old shepherd's hut where there was an old corn bin and I thought he couldn't get out. When I went back next day he was still there so I gave him some bits to make another nest. Then I took this ol' canary cage up to the wood and put 'im in it. I even went to Petersfield and bought 'im some nuts.

'Eventually I noticed that *he* was getting unusually fat and was astonished when four young ones appeared. But I reared 'em successfully. Then the Forestry Commission got to know of it and one of their men came all the way from Scotland to see me, as dormice were never known to breed in captivity. He wanted to buy 'em, but I said you can have the young but I'll keep the old one. Fred Courtier, of the Forestry Commission in the New Forest, was given the job of lookin' after them in a big aviary.

'Not long after I was trimmin' away in the wood, where I sometimes put bags in pop-holes. I noticed one of these bags 7ft up in a fork and when I climbed up there was a nest inside it with a dormouse fast asleep. It turned out to be a male, so I thought, all right now, I'll put it with my female, which had then been with me for two years. So I did, but a few weeks later the male became thin and died. Then the female went thin, got watery eyes and she died too. I don't know why.'

Don also has some very special memories of mice during the record-breaking freeze of winter 1962–3. 'Whenever I snared and skinned foxes the mice was so hungry they'd come out and strip the car-casses bare. They even ate the plastic off the tops of the shock absorber springs to get at and eat the grease in my new Ford Anglia estate.

'That winter the snow came on Boxing Day and lasted till 3 March in Sussex. We were cut off all that time because we lived a mile from the main road, and we couldn't even shoot till the end of January, when we had a keepers' and beaters' day and shot 300 cocks. I still managed a nine-mile feed round on foot every day. Although I kept making tracks in the snow they constantly filled up with new drifts.'

The snow was exceptionally thick in 1947 too, when Don had to go down to the pens to dig the birds out. 'They were sealed in under the boughs.' And years later, in Dorset, the snow was so heavy part of the keepers/beaters shooting party had to stay over.

Don receives his 40-year long-service award from the Queen in 1989

The weather also played havoc on the Shaftesbury estate during the hurricanes of 1987 and 1989. 'We lost thousands of trees – mostly beech and oak.' This was a major setback for such a fine shoot, which once had five double-gun days and has often hosted whole clutches of notables, from ambassadors to noblemen such as the Duke of Gloucester and Prince Michael. And big names once expected big bags. 'Our best was over 700 – on a January cock day!' But Don's main concern has been to provide quality rather than mere quantity.

When it comes to organising a shoot day Don has been a grand master, leaving no detail to chance. He even makes sure that he faces his Land-Rover away from a drive, 'as I've seen birds go through the screens'. But although he grew up in the old school of keepering he never dwelt in the past. In recent years he has been as familiar with walkie-talkies, radio-tagging of game and the management of let days, as the old skills of mixing your own pheasant feed.

I think one of the reasons why Don has been such a good provider of shooting is that he has truly enjoyed participating in the sport himself. He wants others to experience the many thrills which have come his way, whether it's ambushing the wide variety of wild duck which still drop into the Dorset estate or a day with the highest of pheasants. His favourite is grouse shooting in Scotland. 'It's the air, the company, the atmosphere. A few high birds, a few crossers, one behind you. Have a good lunch, go back in the afternoon; then home to wash up and reflect on the day over a glass of whisky. You can't beat it. But I never shoot my own pheasants.'

But like so many other sportsmen, Don has found that, 'the older you get the less you want to shoot things'. This is not to say that Don is turning away from the gameshooting scene. Indeed, with age the company of kindred spirits becomes even more important, but the emphasis changes to enjoyment in helping others. And few keepers could ever give up their gundogs. Don gets 'a lot of satisfaction from picking-up, and I like shooting in trials, but not competing. A keeper can't have a trial dog. A good trial dog is no good for vermin control or drivin' in.'

Don had his first golden retriever at the age of twelve and has had between one and five ever since. Currently he has four and, traditionally, all their names begin with S – Scud, Snipe, Spark and Shooter.

In his day, Don was a champion claypigeon shooter, his most important wins including the South of England Sporting Championship. At the Gallyon's gamekeepers' shoot in 1965 he won the silver partridge for the best aggregate score, as well as the coveted silver and golden pheasants. He still enjoys a clayshoot and has an impressive collection of guns.

Despite all his arduous duties, Don has always found time to help others and to further the sport he has loved. He has assisted Game Conservancy researchers in field projects and is now a regional representative of the British Association for Shooting and Conservation's Gamekeeper Services Committee, having been treasurer of the old Gamekeepers' Association.

Clearly, every corner of the 6,500-acre Dorset estate (it was 8,000 acres when he started) holds special memories for Don. As you walk around with him he maintains a running commentary. 'Now this drive here – the Mental Home – is so called because workers from the mental home came to repair the lunch hut there, and one of them put a sign on it. And over there, on the Harley Gap drive,

I remember the year I came here we killed more than 400 hares the first day and 200-odd the second. But in the second year, after they started putting Gramoxone on the stubbles to kill weeds, we shot only seventy by lunch-time on the first day. So we left them alone for seven years. Out of that seventy in year two, mortality was so high that only one hare was four years or over. The Game Conservancy's research department examined their eyes to determine their age.'

Don always used to catch-up his own breeding stock, from the second week in February. 'We used big, permanently fed catchers and caught up to 200 in one in a day. Sometimes we had a change of blood with pheasants from other estates, but you had to be so careful. When they were first put to wood, we used troughs for two or three weeks, but gradually introduced hand-feeding, with wheat, maize and pellets till nine or ten weeks.'

Not surprisingly, Don believes that, 'the best keepers have it bred in and must be dedicated. They can't be off motorbike racin' on a Saturday and Sunday. Their wives must take an interest [Don's second wife Liz will endorse this!] and accept that you work seven days a week, at all hours, in all weathers. You've got to be a good walker and a good Shot for vermin control. Trouble is today you don't get the good trappers: so many don't bother and just put down another thousand birds to make up the losses. I don't agree with that.'

Don's son, Colin, has followed him into the keepering profession but has found the life much more traumatic in an increasingly cost-conscious world. 'You'd have to be damn lucky even to find a job nowadays', Don stresses. 'But if a lad's really

Lord Shaftesbury thanks Don for his long service

keen, my advice is to get friendly with a good keeper and be prepared to put in a lot of voluntary work.'

'But how would an employer spot a good beatkeeper among so many applicants nowadays?' I asked Don. 'Easy,' he replied. 'First thing, shake 'im by the hand. If it's smooth he's no good, but if it's rough then you know he's a good trapper. But a successful shoot's all about teamwork too, with good keepers, good beaters and good pickers-up.' Don Ford may no longer be head of that team, but you can rest assured that he will be a valuable member of it for many seasons to come.

APPROPRIATELY NAMED

HARRY STARLING

NORFOLK AND OXFORDSHIRE

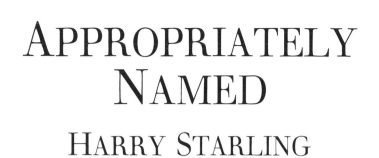

They say that birds of a feather flock together, but never was the saying more appropriate than in the case of Harry Starling. When he started keepering in 1945, not only did he join his headkeeper father Jack, but also his brother Tom. And his roost was aptly provided by Ronald Tree, the owner of Ditchley Park estate, Oxfordshire. In later years at Ditchley Harry also worked with a farm manager named Bullock and a forester called Woodhams.

Christened Henry Knight Starling, Harry was born on 18 June 1929, at Pond Hills, near Holt in Norfolk, where his father Jack was headkeeper. His grandfather and father's two brothers were also keepers, but even without this branch of the family, Starlings were thick on the ground in that neck of the woods.

At that time Jack Starling occasionally loaded for Ronald Tree when he came up to Blickling Hall, and in 1934 the distinguished keeper was tempted to join the Oxfordshire estate. Harry was then only five but clearly remembers being scared of encountering 'those terrible foxes, because we had none where we were in Norfolk.

Harry Starling's grandfather, Thomas (holding pheasants, left), in about 1896, at his home on Thomas Cook's estate, Senowe Park, Guist, Norfolk

Jack Starling did not retire from keepering until he was 84, and was mentioned in despatches in the Great War

'Ditchley was all oak and hazel woods and hadn't been shot for ages. There used to be about 5,000 acres and before the war there was a big gang of men on the land and in the woods.'

Harry had a one-and-a-half-mile walk to Enstone school, 'where I did quite well'. He was already helping father on the rearing field and 'liked to drive the horse. I also remember we used to pray for cold nights so that the pheasants came in early and we didn't have to stay out too late shutting them up.

'The estate got its first shoot vehicle – an old Ford Thames van – in 1943, but father couldn't drive. One day my brother was home on leave and he said to me, "I'll teach you and you teach dad". So that's what we did.' Subsequently, Harry became very interested in mechanics, taking up the trade when he did his National Service, also becoming a keen motor cyclist in the Army.

'I left school and started full-time as an underkeeper with father at the age of sixteen in 1945. He was very strict. There was no rearing allowed during the war and for a few years after, but there was plenty of wild game and most of the work was just keeping vermin down.'

Jack Starling was born in 1888 and fought in the Great War, being mentioned in dispatches for conspicuous gallantry in 1918. During World War II he became a sergeant in the Home Guard. Harry recalls 'the night they thought the Germans had landed. We heard stones being thrown at the window and looked out to see the officer, who was the estate agent, standing under a tree with a revolver in his hand. At that, father darted off to the observation point on the top of Ditchley mansion. Real *Dad's Army* stuff.

'During the war the estate often held joint shoots with Blenheim. No feeding

of the birds was allowed officially, but in those days there was always a bit left round the edges of the fields.

'Churchill used to come to Ditchley, 'When The Moon Was High', which was the title of a book written by Ronald Tree, but he did not shoot. He was supposed to be safe there but we always thought it odd that nearby there was one of those false runways with lights on. We also had the Americans camped on Ditchley – they liked a squirrel or two and we always got a few candies in return.

'David Niven shot there quite a lot during the war. His first wife was in the Tree family. I loaded for him and he was quite a good Shot. Sometimes we used to walk the hedgerows for a whole day. We also used to get Ed Murrow, the American news reporter.'

During the 1940s Harry earned about £2 10s, 'and I remember that father really thought he was in the money when he got £5 a week just after the war – and he had six children!'

In 1947 Harry started to take an active part in the organisation of the annual Venables' Gamekeepers' Clay Pigeon Shoot at Ditchley Park. During the 1950s he was a regular at the Gallyon's Gamekeepers' Shoot in Cambridge, winning the silver and golden pheasant trophies, the latter twice.

Ditchley was sold to the Earl of Wilton in 1949, and in 1953 to Sir David Wills. 'During the late 1960s and early 1970s the Duke of Leinster took the shooting and I had eight happy years working for him.' Jack Starling retired in 1972 and died in 1983 at the age of ninety-one. He was succeeded as headkeeper by his eldest son, Harry's brother Tom, who retired in 1987 and died on Christmas Eve 1989.

There was no shooting at Ditchley from 1976 so Harry had to work on the farm

The keepers at Ditchley Park in 1936

there. 'But in winter there was too much clickin' the heels for me, so in 1979 I came here to Kiddington [Oxfordshire], as headkeeper for the late Sir Lawrence Robson.' Harry succeeded Les Stone, who followed in the formidable footsteps of Lawrence Fisk, headkeeper 1919–67.

Today, the Honourable Maurice Robson recalls how lucky they were the day Harry came to them. 'He has produced some memorable shooting with a consistent average of 250–300 birds per day throughout the season. His team of beaters are a true reflection of his own skills: friendly, well-disciplined and keen. Beaters' Day on the last Saturday each season is as eagerly awaited as the annual dinner. There is a rumour that the waiting list to beat at Kiddington rivals the list for places at Eton! Harry is given strong support by his immediate family – his wife Heather, his brother Maurice, and his son Paul, who breeds Longhorn cattle at Rousham and comes beating at Kiddington. His daughter Susan is married to a keeper.

'Complementary to his skills as a true countryman, Harry is a brilliant mechanic. There is no part of a Land-Rover which he cannot repair.' Indeed, Harry keeps two on the road and proudly declares that they have never been to a garage. However, this does mean that everyone brings him things to mend!

Harry received his long-service medal in 1991 and still rules the roost as strictly as 'Old Man Starling'. 'I never let beaters bring dogs – you can only drive pheasants with men and sticks. When I came here there was one chap had five Jack Russells – it was like the Heythrop Hunt coming through. He never came again.'

At 'only' sixty-four, Harry Starling is a relatively young bird and if he decides to retire at the customary age the sporting community will lose a valuable servant.

During the 1950s Harry enjoyed great success at the annual Gallyon's gamekeepers' shoot

ACKNOWLEDGEMENTS

My very special thanks go to the stars of the book—the keepers themselves—and to their families, for their most generous help and hospitality and for lending me their precious old photographs. Secondly, I am indebted to Phil Murphy for producing another delightfully evocative set of illustrations. My thanks also to Ken Stott and Ken Beattie, and gamekeepers Walter Cole, Dave Clark, Alan Edwards, Ian Grindy, Alan Sephton and Dave Whitby for their excellent leads. Finally, my thanks to editor Sue Hall and the rest of the David & Charles team.

INDEX

Page numbers in *italics* refer to illustrations